TAMRA RYAN

FOLLOWSHIP

16 LESSONS TO BECOME
A LEADER WORTH FOLLOWING

FOLLOWSHIP
16 LESSONS TO BECOME A LEADER WORTH FOLLOWING
TAMRA RYAN
Copyright © 2025 Tamra Ryan
All Rights Reserved.

For more information: Tamra@tamraryan.com
ISBN (paperback): 978-1-962280-69-3
ISBN (ebook): 978-1-962280-70-9

Contents

About Women's Bean Project

From 2003 to 2025 I was the CEO of an employment social enterprise called Women's Bean Project (WBP), located in Denver, Colorado. The Bean Project, as it is also called, is a food manufacturer that employs women experiencing chronic unemployment. The products consist of a variety of dry food mixes—the first product was a bean soup mix, the genesis of the company's name—as well as baking mixes, spice blends, and a variety of delicious snacks and candies, which are distributed across the US and online through some of the country's largest retailers.

But the business isn't the Bean Project's primary purpose. WBP believes all women have the power to transform their lives through employment, so they hire women who have typically not ever held a job longer than a year, though their average age is thirty-seven. These women usually have long histories of addiction, incarceration, homelessness, or domestic violence. Their past experiences have created barriers to getting and keeping employment, which is why they apply to WBP. Women are hired for a transitional job that lasts six to nine months. During their time as employees, they work in food production, making all the products, as well as in the shipping and fulfillment department, ensuring those products get to customers across the country. The physical part of the job is called the "bean job" and women spend 70 percent of their paid time doing it.

The Bean Project provides women work experience to learn basic job readiness skills, as well as helping them focus on their psychosocial barriers to employment. Women spend 30 percent of their time working on themselves, which is called the "you job." During this portion of their time, they get connected to resources for housing and childcare. They are supported while they develop plans for their sobriety, learn skills for healthy relationships, and improve their communication and conflict resolution skills. They also work on improving math and reading, learn planning and organizing, and practice basic computer skills.

WBP is an anomaly in the business world. They are a business, with product sales creating more than 50 percent of the organization's revenue. They are also a human services organization, and they raise grants and donations to support the program activities that make each woman's experience unique to her while she is focused on transforming her life. WBP makes products to create jobs and employ women, but the products aren't the point. The business also creates the opportunity for the women to make new lives for themselves.

The Bean Project is not a place women go to stay the same. It is a place for each woman to create a new life for herself and her family, one where she maintains employment and experiences the dignity of supporting herself and her children. After completing her time at WBP, each woman goes on to a career-focused, entry-level job in the community. These jobs have opportunities for advancement and benefits, and her employer cares that she comes to work because they are invested in her. This will likely be the first time she has had a job such as this. A year after completing the program at WBP, over 95 percent of women are still employed.

My role as the CEO of this organization was the job of a lifetime and gave me an opportunity to learn and grow. I figured out who I was and who I wanted to be as a leader. As I look back on my experiences, there are many times I wish I'd had someone to advise me, challenge me, and support me. This book is a reflection of what I wish I'd known sooner.

Introduction

We are in a leadership crisis. Across sectors and around the world, our belief in leaders has been in steady decline for more than a decade, and we have reached a critical state. People don't trust their leaders, a fact that is corroborated by research. The Global Agenda Councils conducted a survey in which it identified the issues expected to have the greatest impact on the world in the coming twelve to eighteen months. Eighty-six percent of respondents identified a leadership crisis as their top issue because leaders are mired in factions and not doing enough to solve the big problems of the world.[1]

In the midst of the COVID pandemic, the economic crisis, and the global outcry about systemic racism that followed, another important indicator of people's trust, the Edelman Trust Barometer, revealed an accelerated and widespread distrust in societal institutions and leaders around the world. Followers are requiring leaders to work to rebuild trust across sectors including business, government, and nongovernmental organizations (NGOs, which are commonly referred to as nonprofit organizations in the US), as well as the media. The declining belief in leadership around the world means not even one sector is truly trusted to do what is right.[2]

Though all trust scores have dropped, in 2022 the Edelman Trust Barometer shared that people's trust in business now outscores trust in government and other sectors.[3] Those surveyed reported feeling that businesses are the only institutions believed to be able to address societal problems such as climate change, economic inequities, and workforce reskilling to ensure economic mobility, while also providing trustworthy information. Societal leadership is now considered a core function of business, and trust has become more localized, i.e., I trust *my* coworkers and *my* CEO. Followers want their CEO to speak out on issues, to be personally visible when public policy is being addressed, and to be outspoken about what the company has done to benefit society and shape societal conversations. By contrast, both government and the media are viewed as divisive because they are seen as fueling the cycle of distrust.

Pew Research Center has further documented societal distrust. In research published in 2019, Pew indicated two-thirds of people in the US think their fellow Americans have little to no confidence in the government. Because of its partisan factions, the general belief is that the government has let down its citizens. The Pew report confirms that this lack of trust and the crisis in leadership extends to religious organizations and media. Over the past decade, the media has lost credibility because of the prevalence of news that seems partisan or untrustworthy. Even trust in NGOs, which were historically more trusted than other organizations, has dipped to second place after business. Nearly half of Americans believe nothing can be relied on as it used to be.[4]

Why is this lack of trust a problem? Distrust leads to a lack of confidence, and confidence is essential for economies to function. Without public trust, societies are unable to effectively respond to public health crises, as witnessed during the recent pandemic. A high level of trust is connected with less violence in communities and more economic security. The UN secretary-general warns that distrust threatens to undermine progress toward the world's Sustainable Development Goals, targets that have been set by the UN to decrease poverty and suffering and increase empowerment across the globe.[5] The cycle of distrust threatens societal stability and the lack of strong, inspirational leadership is making it worse.

All institutions that help our society function are built on a foundation of trust. Supporters of NGOs must trust that the organizations they give to are deploying the funds to do the work they say they will and in the way donors expect of them. Often, the supporters are unable to witness the work firsthand and must have faith their gifts are used as intended and the outcomes are being reported accurately and with integrity. For NGOs, the amount of money donated, the numbers of donors, and the retention rate of those donors can serve as proxies for how much trust and confidence supporters have in the organization.

Missteps by religious leaders have created a wariness in followers. Too often, leaders who try to maintain the moral high ground end up on the slippery slope toward loss of credibility when their actions don't match the values they are holding their followers accountable to. We have seen this happen with numerous religious leaders, from Catholic priests to ministers of megachurches.

Whether we look at the media or politicians, our respect for leaders has plummeted. We feel duped by those who say anything to gain our support but do nothing to follow through. Most recently, we witnessed examples during the COVID pandemic. For the first time in at least a half century, we were all being affected by something grave and were looking to our leaders to guide us. Yet too many of these leaders were mired in posturing, providing misinformation, and politicking in ways that felt counterproductive to a solution. Today, many people are wondering where the leaders who might inspire us to follow them have gone. They puzzle over what is missing from those in charge that has left them feeling flat and uninspired.

This widespread dearth of trust makes the case for doing leadership differently. It's time to turn the focus away from what leaders want to give and toward what followers are seeking from their leaders—what entices people and enlists them to join the leader in accomplishing great things. I call this new way of leading "followship."

What followers expect from their leaders has shifted. Effective leadership is no longer the command-and-control style of previous generations when the leader was a singular, great individual whom followers did not question. Gone are the days when everyone looked to the individual at the top of the organizational chart to give directives to the people positioned beneath them. Followers have been burned by leaders who required unquestioned authority. They no longer want their leader to save them from having to think or worry about the issues facing the company. No one is seeking hierarchical leadership anymore.

To start on the path toward followship, we must begin by understanding what followers are looking for from their leaders. Today we look to CEOs to take the lead on policy, such as climate change, reskilling, and diversity, as well as expecting them to be a model for long-term thinking. As an NGO leader, I have learned how essential it is for me to meet these expectations of engagement; however, I wonder how many CEOs in other sectors realize what is being asked of them. Not only are leaders expected to lead companies, but followers also want them to take a stand in areas where government has disappointed them. Leaders in business and NGOs are expected to behave as a unifying force in society.

Not surprisingly, many leaders are caught in the gap between where they currently sit because of their training, background, and role models, and where their followers expect them to be. For too long, leaders have been encouraged to think about their own success in an individual way rather than as a big-picture, collective concept. Boards and the public tend to focus on the leader's accomplishments. They give accolades to the individual at the top to celebrate success, encouraging them to continue their inward focus with no concern for soft skills such as values alignment, self-awareness, and integrity. The leaders haven't been taught or encouraged to think about how their actions might change for the benefit of systems and society because markets and shareholders reward them for a short-term mindset even when long-term thinking would be better for all.

Leaders are learning the hard way that the relationship between them and their follower has been democratized. Followers now understand their power to choose whether or not to stay with the leader. We need only look at the Great Resignation that occurred in 2021 to see evidence of this disconnect. Followers have realized they are looking for leaders who align with their values and who can serve as a compass to guide their actions. They want their leaders to have the courage to look in the mirror, the integrity to accept what others see, and the gumption to take action to rectify their gaps. And they are willing to show their displeasure by leaving the leader to find new employment.

Followers want their leaders to see them as more than a means to an end. They want to know the leader is concerned for them and their thoughts and feelings. They want someone who is values-driven—who will communicate those values and stay true to them, even when it is hard. Followers want to be heard and be part of the decisions driving their organization.

Even when leaders cannot name these pressures, they feel them. Recently, I was with a group of female CEOs. As we sat around a set of tables configured in a circle, catching up on our recent personnel experiences, the conversation veered toward lamenting the challenges of leading employees. As we talked about recruiting, hiring, and retaining employees, many of the CEOs were frustrated by their feelings that nothing ever seemed to be enough. "People just don't want to work hard anymore," one CEO said. "No matter what I do, it isn't enough," said another. A third shared that she had nothing more to give. Each of these leaders sat in the gap between what they thought they knew about leading and the shift in their employees' expectations. Their pain was real and existential, and I suspect their employees were feeling the same.

We are living in a time of paradox for leaders. Jim Rohn, an American entrepreneur and motivational speaker, said it well: "The challenge of leadership is to be strong, but not rude; be kind, but not weak; be bold, but not a bully; be thoughtful, but not lazy; be humble, but not timid; be proud, but not arrogant; have humor, but without folly."[6] Phew.

We put our leaders on a pedestal and then proceed to pick them apart for their inadequacies. We are certainly surrounded by many egocentric leaders; look no further than our most prominent tech entrepreneurs. And no wonder—we created them by perpetuating the myth of the single, brilliant leader who changes the world. The problem is that when they betray our trust, we resent being stuck looking up at them.

And therein lies one of the paradoxical challenges of leadership: leading a company is simultaneously about the leader and not about the leader. People often chose to support Women's Bean Project based on meeting me. This fact was essential to my role as the leader of this NGO: to bring resources into the organization. Yet, I recognized it was never truly about me, and I understood the danger if I began to believe it was. I realized I could never allow my ego to be tied to my position.

But how do leaders balance the notion that leading depends on them yet is not all about them? I believe it requires the leader to get comfortable sitting between an inward focus on themself and an outward focus on followers and the environment. The inward focus requires the leader to keep their own ego, emotions, and needs in check while focusing on others' egos, emotions, and needs. It requires both self-awareness—being grounded in the present reality and how they are being perceived—while also looking out to the horizon to create a vision that will inspire others to join them on the journey to a better future. Followship happens when leaders engage and listen to the people they wish to inspire and build trust with.

I served as the CEO of WBP for twenty-two years. This means I had plenty of opportunities to make mistakes and learn from them. In this time, I embraced the responsibilities and nuances of my position and came to understand that leading is not something you do. A leader is someone you are. To me, there is little more magical than watching a team of people, led by a leader who has captured their imagination with a vision, engaged their trust with integrity, motivated them with courage, and created enduring bonds as a result of their emotional intelligence, work to accomplish things they might never have thought possible.

My aim in sharing with you the keys to what I've learned about followship is to save you time and help you avoid making the same mistakes I made. Throughout the book you will find examples of my own experiences and observations about what has allowed me to lead effectively and where my actions have fallen flat. I have also highlighted examples from well-known leaders, chosen because they exemplify a particular lesson well, even if they struggle with other areas of leadership. Other stories highlight opportunities missed by leaders whose followers would have benefited if only the leaders had made different choices.

I learned that the essence of my job as the CEO was in my ability to enlist people to join me in caring about and working to solve the societal problem WBP exists to address. In my role as the CEO, my job was to inspire people to give their time, talent, and treasure to support the Bean Project. After years of observing, researching other leaders, trying strategies, and adapting to the results, I have come to believe that being a leader worth following isn't about any one thing but instead a combination of skills and behaviors. This book is not about doing leadership. It is a guide for being a leader. I hope you can use the examples on your own leadership journey, and I encourage you to take what you need and disregard the rest (or store the lessons away until you need them). As we evolve, what we need to support our leadership skills does too.

As I was researching this book, I conducted interviews with friends, colleagues, and others I had met professionally. I started each interview by asking what I hoped would get to the essence of the idea behind followship: Who in your career has so inspired you that you would crawl through broken glass to follow them? At first, I was not sure this was the right question, but I quickly noted one of two things occurred immediately upon asking the question. Either the person being asked would say, "I have never worked with a leader like that." Or the interviewee would get a dreamy look in their eye and say they knew exactly who the person was and what they had done to be remembered so fondly. Through their recollections, I began to see a pattern and was able to condense these memorable behaviors into four characteristics that make a leader worth following: vision creation, integrity, courage, and emotional intelligence.

A leader worth following leads the creation of the vision for their organization. The vision is created because the leader is constantly listening to and integrating information from the environment with an idea of what the future could look like. The leader not only understands their own company and industry but also has a sense of the external world in which the company operates, along with the rapid social changes affecting their followers' behaviors and psyches. As the vision is being created, the leader must have the ability to connect the dots between all the collected information. They must then be able to relay the vision clearly while enlisting followers to come along on the journey to a future in which the vision is realized. When this is done well, followers want to join the leader; they begin repeating back the elements of the vision that are sticky and resonate with them. The vision becomes shared and no longer belongs only to the leader.

Integrity is an essential building block of trust. As Brené Brown, an American professor, social worker, author, and podcast host expressed, trust is a bank, and a leader is always making deposits. In her book *The Anatomy of Trust*, Brown wrote about the essential elements needed to achieve and keep trust, including being consistently reliable by doing what one says they are going to over and over again, being accountable and owning one's mistakes, and being clear on one's values and practicing them. A leader with integrity says what they mean and means what they say. Followers appreciate their consistency and know they can take this leader at their word.

A leader worth following is courageous. Courage in a leadership context means choosing to do the hard things over what is easy. A leader with courage overcomes their fear and learns to be okay with discomfort. Courage is shown by being vulnerable—admitting one's weaknesses and errors in a way that builds trust and loyalty. It requires the knowledge that covering up mistakes is not courageous and leads to a loss of trust. A brave leader also understands that it takes a huge amount of courage to apologize genuinely because of the humility one must have.

And finally, leaders worth following are emotionally intelligent. They are relatable because they focus their leadership on soft skills versus hard. They lead with empathy, kindness, and compassion. They are more human and approachable and have made the shift from the autocratic, selfish model of leading to one that is collective, in touch, and inspirational in a way that followers want today. The leader with emotional intelligence makes all team members feel valued and as though they belong to the team and are doing work that is larger than themselves. These qualities inspire followers and enlist them to join the leader on the journey to accomplishing great things together.

Even if they are not acutely aware, followship makes or breaks leaders, and leaders make or break organizations. Leaders worth following are powerful because they make followers excited to work together in pursuit of something greater than they could accomplish individually. They feel inspired to be their best selves and are willing to tackle things they never saw themselves capable of before. These followers exist in an environment in which they feel empowered, even when the leader is not present, because they feel they have the skills needed and know what to do.

In this book, with the help of sixteen lessons, you will learn about followship: the art of inspiring others to follow you. You will learn about the differences between managing and leading, and about the ways of showing up that get others excited, inspired, and motivated to join you, the leader, on the quest to accomplishing great things. You will learn what many followers already know: that leaders are leading all the time, well or poorly, with intention or not. Together we will examine which leader behaviors inspire and motivate followers and which fall flat. You will learn that in order to truly excel at leadership, you must be excellent at followship.

Since I was young, others labeled me as a leader. I ran for office numerous times throughout my school years, culminating in being elected student body president in my senior year of high school. I attended leadership camps and was chosen for a prestigious leadership program for my undergraduate years at the University of Colorado in Boulder. I never questioned the label or wondered what it meant to be a leader. This leader label followed me into the world of work as I rose relatively quickly to a director level within the first organization at which I was employed.

Despite this experience, I didn't understand what it meant to lead until after I became the CEO of WBP. And even then, it took some time to embrace the idea of what it meant, and more importantly, why anyone might want to follow me.

I recall the time when I felt ready to lead a company. I had worked for several leaders who had not inspired me. I followed them because of their titles—president, owner, CEO—and because it was a requirement of my position. I learned quickly and repeatedly that if I disagreed with the leader, I would lose, because what they mandated was required. I felt there was a difference between following someone because I had to rather than because I was inspired to. And so I took the leap and applied to become the CEO of a company. I now realize that I didn't know what it meant to be a leader worth following. At that time I viewed leadership as equal parts cheerleader, enforcer, and role model. I believed if I was enthusiastic enough, I could get people to come along with me. If the energy in the room was flat, it was my job to improve it.

Maybe these strategies were valuable. But they didn't consider the follower's viewpoint. That is the crux of the issue.

So often, when we become leaders, we forget what it was like to be a follower, particularly if we have never experienced a leader worth following.

During my tenure as the CEO of the Bean Project, the organization grew tenfold from the size it was when I started, which caused my job to change—but revenue wasn't the only reason for the change. The job changed because I changed. I progressed from being a manager who called herself a leader to truly embodying the position. I matured personally and professionally and developed perspective I wasn't able to see when I first took on the role. My understanding of the job, how to occupy the position, and how to show up have all evolved as I have learned what leadership means and what it means to be a leader who inspires others to join me in a quest to address the challenges faced by women in communities across the country.

While working at WBP, I became well-known in the field of social enterprise. I had opportunities to speak to audiences around the world and frequently to women's groups, especially in male-dominated industries where women struggle to find their voice and power; places where these women are working to embrace their unique ability to inspire followers.

The skills I have learned have helped me create a platform of thought leadership that now extends to policy discussions where I have had the opportunity to converse with policymakers and scholars influencing national issues.

Most importantly, I have embraced the responsibilities and nuances of leading. I understand leading is not something I do, it's who I am. This mindset is rewarded constantly. I've been able to watch my team work together to accomplish our goals and realize the vision we created. I think we all aspire to be this kind of leader.

This book is for anyone who has wondered why they have felt uninspired or disappointed by the leaders they have encountered. It's for leaders who want to be better by learning from leaders who inspire others. I believe this book will resonate with leaders who know the old way of leadership no longer works and are ready to commit to being a better version of themselves for their followers.

This is not a one-size-fits-all approach or another book about leadership from the leader's perspective. It isn't a how-to in the sense of "just follow these instructions and you will be a great leader." It's not written from an all-knowing place nor is it a list of rules that must be followed as the only path to success, because followship is about nuance and art.

This book walks through ways leaders can inspire their followers, build trust, and accomplish great things together. Working toward becoming a leader worth following doesn't require you to master each lesson. As humans, we each have strengths and weaknesses. You may have already learned some of these lessons; others may elude you.

This book makes the case for bringing humanity back to leadership, raising the bar for ourselves, and demanding more of our leaders. But before we dig in to the lessons learned around the four essential characteristics of vision, integrity, courage, and emotional intelligence, let's address an issue I have seen many new leaders struggle with: making the transition from managing to leading.

Chapter 1

From Doing to Being

How do you start each day? Do you look at the appointments on your calendar and the list of things you need to get done? Do you imagine how you want to show up for your day over a cup of coffee or as you are exercising? Do you think about who you wish to be?

I belong to a group of women presidents and CEOs from a variety of companies. We gather over lunch each month to discuss our challenges, both business and personal. At the beginning of each meeting, we share updates and choose a topic we can workshop to help one of us address a nagging issue. Though we are workshopping a problem one person brings, it is usually a concern several women in the group share. Not long ago, at one of our meetings, one CEO lamented how little her team seemed to be at their desks working. She felt they didn't put in the hours she had when she was working her way to success. She asked our group what we thought she should do about it, wondering aloud what would be required to motivate people to work as hard as she does. Around the large conference table, each of my fellow CEOs shared their perspectives. My turn came second to last, and I asked whether she was looking to be a manager or a leader. When she looked at me quizzically, I said a manager would be focused on how much time everyone's butts were in their seats producing work. But a leader would be focused on how well the team was coming together to accomplish the mission of the organization. If the mission is being accomplished, the amount of time the butts were in seats would matter less. Mic drop. The person after me merely said, "I can't add anything to Tamra's comments."

When someone asks me how to make the transition from manager to leader, it's usually not asked with a direct question. In fact, I wonder if those who are struggling to make the shift understand what they are struggling with. I recall a time at a women's conference, after I'd finished my talk about the power of compassionate leadership, a sharply dressed woman approached me and earnestly asked, "How do I find the balance between being responsible for the people in my department and making sure the work gets done?" She shared she had recently been promoted to lead her division in a technology company. She was now reporting to the CEO and responsible for the success of the department as measured by their customer ratings, efficiency and speed in solving technology issues, and keeping her departmental costs under control. "All the people who now work for me are men, and several of them are disrespectful and ignore my direction," she lamented. She wondered aloud how she could establish her authority and show them she knew as much about their software as they did.

I was struck by this last part. As the leader of her division, it didn't seem to me she needed to be the best programmer or know the most about their company's technology solution. In fact, by focusing too much on the work of the people she was now responsible for, she was missing the fact that she had just been promoted to lead them. Since she was accustomed to working side by side with the people who she was now charged with leading, she was finding her new role elusive. While she understood her role had changed, she struggled to understand what it meant to lead her team, making her feel overwhelmed and lost. She was questioning whether or not she had the skills to do the job, saying, "I feel like I'm not qualified to run this division."

I asked her a few questions because I was curious to hear what her company's goals were and how she was enlisting her team to do their part in accomplishing them. I asked how she typically spent her time and how she checked in with her new direct reports—the ones who were not following her. As she shared what she did during a typical week, I learned she spent a majority of her time being worried about the team's output. She spent a lot of time trying to figure out how to be perceived as nice so they would like her and do what she asked of them. And, she was living in the moment, running from meeting to meeting, constantly in reaction mode and rarely stopping to think or plan.

As she described her days, I couldn't help but feel her frenetic stress. The job was managing her rather than the other way around. I made a couple of suggestions I hoped would set her on a path to making her job feel more doable. I advised her to get clarity on the company's overarching goals and, more specifically, how her team would contribute to the company's success. Her time should be spent enlisting her team in helping the company succeed, I said, not in making sure she was supervising each person. I also suggested she consider how she could become more mindful, starting each day with intention rather than letting her calendar bounce her from meeting to meeting without time to reflect and lead. Finally, I encouraged her to stop worrying so much about being liked. Her job was not to be popular with her team but to lead them to accomplish the company's objectives.

I have witnessed even seasoned leaders struggle to wrangle their calendars and to-do lists. They look to other leaders for the secret formula that will decrease the feelings of overwhelm that are due to what feels like unrelenting demands on their time. Leaders have the sense they have to do all their old work plus the new work of leading. Since leading a company is a lonely role, rarely is someone present to help the leader navigate the challenges they face. Leaders believe they are just expected to know how to lead. This makes them reticent to speak up, and instead, they try to overcome their feelings of inadequacy by working more and more hours. Not only does this rarely work, it creates an emotional toll that can prove unsustainable.

In a typical career progression, one starts as an individual contributor, having responsibility for knowledge and providing work output to others, such as analysis and reports. The next step for a worker rising up the ranks is to be given responsibility for managing individual contributors. In this scenario, the employee often continues to make their own individual contribution, but company leaders look to the manager to be responsible for the work output of the collective. Subsequently, there may be increasing levels of responsibility for these managers, but fundamentally, they are still managing.

Eventually, a few managers become leaders. In this new role, they are no longer responsible for managing the individual or aggregate performance of individuals. Now they are responsible for the organization—and people and organizations cannot be "managed" in the same way. Organizations function when individual contributors are working collectively. Leaders who were previously very confident and qualified managers can get overwhelmed by self-doubt. Having never thought about how leading is different than managing, they believe everyone else has leadership figured out and that they are impostors who will be exposed for their lack of understanding of their new leadership role.

When I became the leader of Women's Bean Project, it was the first time in my career that I could be busy all day yet have nothing to show for it. I was accustomed to creating work output, such as presentations, reports, or other tangible evidence of my effort. Initially, I didn't understand this was a reflection of how my role had changed. I was still in the doing mindset.

Though my role had changed to leading, the staff I had inherited was small at that time, so I took over marketing responsibilities too. Marketing was my professional background before arriving at the Bean Project, so I thought it made sense.

But as I moved further into embracing my CEO role, my marketing skills became less sharp, and I was no longer up to date on the latest online trends. However, I was still good at marketing strategy, like brand building, which I came to realize was more aligned with my CEO role. As the CEO, my purview was larger, and I needed to be focused on high-level strategic thinking that was consistent with our organization's overall vision. Eventually, I was happy to hand off the day-to-day marketing efforts to a manager whose skills were sharper and whose attention was undivided.

Over time, I learned my CEO job consisted of only three things. First, I was responsible for creating a vision and enlisting people to join me in pursuit of that grand plan for the future. Second, I was responsible for bringing resources into the organization. This happened in a variety of ways including fundraising, sales, and human capital, as well as other ways of building awareness by serving as the face of the organization. And third, my job was to help others do their jobs and become the best they could be.

With this clarity of purpose, I prioritized my actions and saw that everything important fell into these three buckets. If I struggled to determine which bucket something might fall into, it was usually because it was not an activity that was truly essential. This regular analysis of my priorities also led me to begin focusing on intentionality.

I learned I operated best when I started each day with a review of my calendar. Besides helping me select my outfit for the day, it also gave me time to ask myself what activities would require special attention or focus. I thought about how I wanted to show up for the people with whom I was meeting that day. Who did I want to be? I found this habit made me think about my purpose as a leader and the people I was leading. It gave me space to ask "Am I committed to their success?" If the answer was yes, then I could think about what that would look like and how I needed to show up. If the answer was no, that required an entirely different mindset to determine why and what I'd like to do about it.

I believe the transition from managing to leading is mastered through intention. In psychology, intentionality is the ability to think and behave in accordance with one's goals. Rather than allowing the day to happen to you, you have the opportunity to decide what kind of leader you wish to be each day. You decide what you hope to accomplish and why. Then you can choose the actions to match these intentions and goals.

Intention comes from being clear about your purpose each day and thoughtful about which actions taken that day tie to the goals and vision you have set for yourself and your organization. An intentional leader does not allow their calendar to drive them because they are deliberate in their thoughts, actions, and interactions. By working with and for team members, without micromanaging their work, you can focus on purposeful action, making conscious decisions rather than thoughtless or careless decisions that are reactive to the situation.

The transition from leader to manager is about being connected to the thing that is bigger than any task, meeting, or report. It's about being connected to the people one is leading and being mindful of their strengths, weaknesses, aspirations, and goals. The people you lead do not need you to do their jobs; they want you to connect their work to the higher purpose. They watch the leader's actions because actions show what the leader believes and values.

One of the skills I've seen leaders struggle with the most is having difficult conversations. In a perfect world, all conversations are intentional, but going into difficult conversations with intentionality means being thoughtful about how I wish to show up, and who I want to be in that conversation in order to support the person while simultaneously being mindful of the higher purpose, larger outcomes, and strategic vision I am responsible for. I find that being clear on my purpose and showing up to my interactions with others accordingly forces me to stay out of the weeds of management.

Intention can also help leaders overcome impostor syndrome. Being focused on what you, as the leader, are responsible for, gives you less time to look in the rearview mirror and wonder how you got to this new role when the management role was so much more familiar and comfortable. Being clear that leadership requires both a focus on the future and the ability to connect the daily work to the organization's strategic goals allows the leader to intentionally create interactions with their team in a way that is removed from management and focused on leadership. With daily practice and positive results from intentional interactions, the doubts recede, and the team moves toward the vision. Remember, managing is about doing. Leading is about being. I do not "do" leading; I am a leader. As long as I am thinking about how to do, I will not be focused on who I wish to be.

Another adjustment I was required to make was resisting the temptation to have the answers. Managers may be expected to have answers about processes and systems. A leader understands they are serving their followers by resisting this temptation. Instead, they ask questions to help the followers, in partnership with the leader, arrive at the answer that best serves the stated goals. We will discuss this more in a future chapter.

Becoming a leader worth following requires a fundamental mindset shift to being more intentional about how we show up. When done well, we move to a mindset of being. This transition doesn't happen overnight, and it won't happen without intention. What might your days look like if you took some time each morning to pause and think about your leadership intentions for the day?

Now that we have talked about the transition from doing to being, let's look at the four characteristics of being a leader worth following—vision, integrity, courage, and emotional intelligence—and the lessons to learn for each.

Chapter 2
The Importance of Vision

Without a vision, a company is like a ship with no agreement among the crew as to its destination. Team members make decisions based on their own priorities and preferences rather than on how their actions affect the larger purpose. Without a vision, it is impossible to know if the organization has the right structure with the right team members in the right seats. Further, followers struggle to know the why behind their work and they disengage. Why should I bring my whole heart to work if there is no purpose that is larger than me?

Nature abhors a vacuum. If there is no vision, team members will find their own meaning, but not collectively. Instead, they work in silos based on their own definition of purpose. The creation and communication of the vision is the first requirement of being a leader worth following. Without vision, the team is rudderless.

The State of Leadership Development, a report produced by Leadership IQ, summarizes the results from surveys of over

21,000 employees who assessed their leaders' effectiveness. Less than half of those surveyed (48 percent) said their leader's vision for the future seemed aligned with the organization's. A leader's vision alignment can account for 25 percent of employees' inspiration to do their best.[7]

Creating vision

My understanding of what it means to create a vision for others to follow began when I became the CEO of Women's Bean Project. I came to the role at a time when the board of directors, select private foundations, and an interim CEO were working to bring the organization through a financial crisis that had almost led to it shuttering the year before. As such, my initial focus was on understanding all aspects of the business, from working on the food production line to evaluating our newly detailed financial statement to attending the classes offered to our program participants—all with the hope that my better understanding would help me identify the issues that needed to be addressed. It was an intellectual endeavor. Armed with my background studying physiology, I understood that an organization is a set of systems, and I was witnessing a bunch of systems that weren't working. I thought that by identifying what wasn't working, I could home in on what needed to be fixed for the survival of the company.

There was no shortage of problems. In fact, I filled a notebook with handwritten bullet points detailing each challenge, resulting in pages upon pages of items to be addressed. I knew

I didn't have the solutions when the challenges emerged, so this list became a work plan of sorts. With such a focus on survival, there was little time for vision development, and as a new leader, I was also not ready to recognize I didn't know what I didn't know. As I began suggesting and implementing changes that, because of my analyses, were obvious to me, I met with resistance from my new teammates as well as community members who through their past donations and volunteerism were invested financially and emotionally in our work. Many had supported the Bean Project for years in a variety of ways or were involved when our founder had started the organization. I found the pushback extremely frustrating. No one was close enough to see what I saw—that many parts of the organization were broken—and no one else was worried about making payroll every two weeks. Surely everyone knew what staying the same looked like: certain doom for this beloved organization.

After many months of feeling unsupported in the changes I was trying to implement, I began to see that it was never going to be my title or a laundry list of problems that would make people believe in me enough to follow me. Instead, I needed to shift my focus from living in the weeds to shaping a dream for a better, more stable future for the organization, while also highlighting the impact we could have if we survived. This was the piece I had been missing. If people didn't understand where we were headed, what success looked like, and why it mattered, why should I expect them to come along on the journey? As leadership guru Simon Sinek says, "People don't buy what you do. They buy why you do it."[8] I had only ever articulated *what* I was asking people to do, never *why* I was asking them to do it. A further revelation was that the why wasn't because of our financial situation but because WBP mattered to the women it served. And it mattered to the community because these women were their neighbors, sisters, and mothers who were raising future community members.

I couldn't assume my motivation to fix the problems the organization faced would motivate my team or Bean Project supporters. The employees had all come together, not for a job, but for a purpose larger than themselves, but we had never discussed it. Out of all the jobs they could have taken, I didn't know why each of them had chosen to work at WBP. I didn't know why the volunteers and donors gave to the Bean Project.

And so, I began asking. I learned we had staff members with histories of substance misuse who had received help to pull their lives together. Some grew up in poverty with single mothers. Others came from the LGBTQ+ community and understood the feeling of being marginalized like the women we served.

A gentleman who had supported the Bean Project for years shared with me that when they were younger, he, his two sisters, and his mother lived in her car when she was between jobs. He was convinced their lives would have been much better if something like WBP had existed for his mother. One donor shared she knew her sister was living on the streets in another city, harming her own body with drugs and sex, and believed if her sister could find something like the Bean Project in the city where she was staying, it would save her life.

My personal why consisted of two parts. My mother had lost both parents before she finished high school. Growing up, I watched her feelings of disempowerment influence her choices and shape her future. She got married and started having children when she was twenty years old. Once she told me she had wanted to be a nurse, but without parents, she was trapped in a life that was devoid of the options that I had just one generation later. Second, I understood that, while my family was not wealthy, I was born with some privilege, and that didn't make me special. Instead, it presented me with a responsibility to help make my community better for others. And for me, making the community better looked like helping women who lacked feelings of empowerment.

The common thread we all shared was that none of us were very far removed from women who felt disempowerment, shame, or social stigma due to their past experiences. We all believed WBP had a solution that changed lives. Armed with the why, I had the kernels of vision articulation.

Articulating the vision

Each of us had personal reasons why we supported or worked at the Bean Project. If I could create a vision that tapped this motivation, we had incredible potential. People want to be inspired and believe their work matters. The CEO's job is to make the connection between the daily work and the higher purpose by intimately understanding the business and also scanning the environment to gather intelligence that affects the business.

The CEO must then connect what might seem to others to be disparate dots and create a vision for a future desired state. The vision I was charged with creating couldn't be based on what I wanted but on what made sense to everyone because we agreed on the larger purpose of our work.

Others may not immediately understand the vision the leader is forming. That is one of the reasons leading can be lonely work. It's also why the leader must invest time in bringing followers along. It's the leader's job to paint the picture of a preferred future that gets followers excited and working toward a purpose larger than themselves. People are inspired by why, not what or how.

In this quest to shape the vision, I saw that the Bean Project could more effectively serve an essential role in helping women transform their lives through employment if we were more clear about our purpose. What began taking shape was a vision for a future in which WBP provided services so effective and far-reaching that each woman who came to us for employment and services was the last in her family to need us. It became clear that the best possible long-term outcome of our work would be for WBP to become unnecessary. I didn't truly believe becoming unnecessary was possible—there were many more applicants to our program than we could hire—but what would it look like if we came to work every day trying to put ourselves out of business?

Immediately I saw the power of enlisting people to join me in executing on this vision. Instead of discussing at length the problems we were seeking to fix, the conversation shifted to articulating what success looked like. I began using the mantra that, among my former team members, I am known for to this day: Start with the end in mind. When a woman successfully completed the nine-month Bean Project employment program, what were the qualities she exhibited that told us she was successful? How did we want people to feel when they supported our organization by giving money or buying products? If we were wildly successful, how would the world be different? In other words, what was our brand promise to the women we served; to the donors and volunteers who contributed their time, talent, and treasure; and to the customers who bought our products?

Vision results

The result was a combined belief and vision statement that drove the organization's work throughout my tenure. It served as the filter for decisions, helped us allocate resources, and shaped how we operate.

Women's Bean Project believes all women have the power to transform their lives through employment. We envision a day when barriers to employment are eliminated, when employers hire based on talent and potential rather than background, when all women who want a second chance can come to the Bean Project and find the community, support, and confidence needed to improve the future for themselves, their families, and the community. We arrive at work each day to provide services so effective and far-reaching that each woman hired at the Bean Project is the last in her family to need us.

There was also a mindset shift among the staff members. The boldness and clarity of the vision inspired them to be open to new ideas. The loneliness I felt in my quest to single-handedly fix the problems abated because we had become a team of people who had set out to improve the organization. The team was invigorated and staff retention grew. We developed a set of shared values that represented our collective why and guided our group pursuit of the vision. As the leader, I still felt responsible, but instead of pulling the rope alone, I was sharing my grasp with a team of people committed to the vision for a brighter future for women experiencing barriers to employment.

Finally, armed with this vision for success, we were able to make decisions and implement change more collectively to ensure the survival of the organization. More donors gave. Foundations supported our work with grants. Product sales grew. Best of all, program completion reached an all-time high and job retention for women one year after completing the Bean Project program exceeded 95 percent. As positive results rolled in, the critics quieted.

As we evolved, my role shifted from merely developing the vision to being responsible for holding onto the vision and communicating it regularly. It no longer belonged only to me, and I wasn't the only one who cared. I was merely the person responsible for enlisting others to come with me. The beauty of creating a compelling vision is that, as it is incorporated into the culture, it belongs to everyone. It becomes something bigger than any one person (and their beliefs and biases) and gets team members to focus on how their contributions are consistent with achieving the vision. It also helps the team focus on what's important and is likely to get them closer to realizing the vision.

It is crucial to understand that a vision is not a road map detailing all the choices that must be made in the future. Instead, it describes an ideal future state to serve as a guide for the team to help them with difficult decisions and keeps everyone focused on the horizon. It's what inspires commitment to the cause. People with a sense of purpose that comes from buying into a clear vision don't have time for drama. They are focused on being their best selves because only then will they be able to be part of the team that realizes the dream. Then, the roadmap is developed collectively through the process of pursuing the vision.

The vision of Steve Jobs

In modern times, it's hard to think of a leader more visionary than Steve Jobs, the late cofounder of Apple. He knew how to paint a picture of the change he wanted to make and how to enlist others to follow him. He dreamed big and was not limited by what had been done before. He elevated the mission of Apple beyond simply building computers to changing consumers' interaction with technology, allowing Apple to become a creative leader in the consumer electronics space. This mission also drove employees to join him in developing leading-edge technology.

As early as 1980, Jobs talked about his vision of a future with computers on every worker's desk, along with a culture in which technology created more opportunities for employees. Apple senior management even sent a memo to all employees that, effective January 1, 1981, there would be no typewriters at Apple, citing that if they believe word processing was "so neat," then they all needed to use it. They were encouraged to prove the typewriter's obsolescence within the company first in order to prove it to customers. Of course, this wasn't the only time Jobs created a vision that predicted the future. By the mid-1980s, he also saw the eventual rise of home computer usage and the use of computers for entertainment.[9]

Jobs had a remarkable ability to anticipate future trends and the needs of consumers. From the development of the first graphical user interface (game-changing for the personal computing industry) to predicting the rise of digital music (transformative for the music industry), his focus on design and the consumer experience truly changed the world. Regardless of the platform, what we see today on our computer desktops is due to Steve Jobs's vision and Apple's development of this technology.

There were several aspects of Steve Jobs's style that helped make him worthy of following, including pushing his team not to worry about the price of their computers and instead make them "insanely great." When it came to taking risks, instead of trying to catch up when Apple got behind its competitors in technological advancements, he pushed the team to leapfrog over what was currently available. Instead of building the capacity for Apple computers to burn music onto CDs as PCs could, they created the iTunes platform and the iPod. He shared with Apple employees his passion for creating an enduring company where people were motivated to make great products. His world-changing vision and tenacity to push back against people who told him that what he wanted to do was impossible made him an incredible role model for a visionary leader worth following. [10]

The ship whose captain communicates the mission of the voyage to the crew increases the chance of success. Leaders will struggle if they don't invest in creating a well-articulated vision and enlist their team to join them. When everyone is clear on the vision, teams believe in the purpose of their work, make decisions well, and accomplish great things like social change and technological innovation.

Learning the necessity of a well-articulated vision is one key step in becoming a leader worth following. Visionary leaders must be dot connectors and proselytizers of the dream. They must be able to keep their eye on the vision despite distractions and be a slinger of hope for followers. These vision lessons are shared in the coming chapters.

Chapter 3
Think Like a Dot Connector

No doubt about it, leading is a noisy business. Everyone has an opinion and wants to share it. We have incredible access to information—to the point of overload. While we can't lead in a vacuum, not all opinions and information are helpful to us as we lead. Listening and filtering are essential parts of the leader's responsibility. A leader who inspires others listens to their team's thoughts, ideas, and passions. This leader is constantly scanning the environment, anticipating where the world is going and how the organization they lead is uniquely positioned to be part of the future state. The leader worth following can connect those dots and create a vision that is both grounded in the current state and inspired by what is possible. It requires living in the present while looking to the future.

But with all this listening and dot connecting, it can be hard to align others' input with the mission of the company and the leader's values. While hearing from others is essential, it can be distracting for the leader of a company without a stated mission or for someone who doesn't have a deep sense of who they are, what they stand for, what their purpose is, and what motivates them—all of which are essential to forming a vision and working toward it.

As discussed in the last chapter, the vision focuses on the future. The mission focuses on the present and what the organization is doing to realize the vision. The values are the attributes and beliefs that will guide the day-to-day work of the organization. Does your organization value innovation? Or have a customer or quality focus? Do you claim to value integrity, sustainability, or fun? Knowing your values or, more importantly, getting clarity on your values, is required before the leader can begin to connect the dots. With clarity, input from the environment that doesn't fit with your vision, mission, and values can be ignored.

I learned that prior to creating or updating the strategic vision at the Bean Project, we had to take the time to revisit the values we claimed to espouse. Typically, the work of considering the updated vision was done at multiple levels within the organization, including staff teams, the leadership team, and the board of directors. It was then my job to connect the dots between what I heard from these groups, what I was witnessing in the community, and what I saw with the women we served.

A key component of vision creation involves leading through the gap between present state versus future desired state. This means the leader is creating a dream of a future state others cannot yet envision. The new vision defines the perfect or preferred future by highlighting the values and hopes of the organization. It serves to inspire and direct followers' energies toward realizing the vision. When done well, a vision is the greatest tool a leader has in enlisting people to follow. It also serves to make the defining of values easier because the better future state highlighted in the vision also provides insight into what the organization values. For instance, the portion of the Bean Project's statement that addressed removing barriers to employment and giving women a second chance spoke to our values of opportunity, self-sufficiency, transformation, empowerment, community, and support.

Revisiting and refining the values was iterative. In one session we affirmed we valued self-sufficiency. In the next group session, we discussed how the value of self-sufficiency showed up in our program services, in our HR practices, or in how we communicated with our stakeholders. If we said we valued self-sufficiency yet couldn't point to ways we espoused the value, we had to question if it was a true value or merely an aspiration. If it was an aspiration we collectively felt strongly about, then we would add the ways we aimed to begin incorporating this value into our vision for the future.

Thinking in systems

Dot connection is really a form of systems thinking. In systems thinking, a leader makes sense of their environment by thinking holistically rather than in parts. Even though they are seeing the parts, they are able to interpret each aspect of complex situations and how each of those aspects relates to the others. Leaders who do this well examine the problem thoroughly before acting, observing events and data, and understanding that everything is interconnected and there are numerous levers that can be pulled to affect change. Leading is about knowing which levers to pull and when.

Big picture or small picture?

It's easy for a leader to get caught up in the day-to-day problems of their organization, spending time with a downward focus, rather than working toward creating the vision. Sometimes this is referred to as the difference between working *in* the business and working *on* the business. This is management, not leadership, and often happens when the leader isn't sure where they are leading the organization. Without the vision as a description of the company's desired future state, it's difficult to face problems head-on. It becomes tempting to work around the challenges rather than addressing them directly and ensuring everyone's actions are aligned toward a larger purpose—the vision. A clear vision helps the team feel confident that it's worth overcoming challenges so they can realize the dream outlined by the vision.

Visionary leaders don't all use the same strategies. Instead, they customize their strategy for the people and organization they are leading. There are leaders who have a vision for how to help their followers do more, go further, be more productive, make customers happier. I think of Tony Hsieh, the former CEO of Zappos, the online shoe retailer. Their core values, which are informed by Hsieh's philosophy of leadership, put them on the map during a time when people were still reluctant to buy shoes online. One of their ten values is "Deliver WOW through service."[11] Delivering WOW not only happens with the customer service team, as might be expected, but also with ensuring every employee in the company is empowered to do something that goes above and beyond what is expected of them. By saying they deliver WOW, they are saying that nothing they do will be average but instead will deliver an extra special feeling.

There are also leaders who create a vision for moving the company to the next chapter or phase of its life cycle. For Women's Bean Project in 2018, this looked like a mantra of "serving more women better." The idea of serving more women and serving them better came out of conversations with the team in which we asked ourselves, "If we could accomplish anything in the next three to five years, what would it be?" When we were having this conversation, things were going well: Our product sales were growing. We were building a bigger donor base. We had received several multiyear, six-figure grants to support our work and growth. Our outcomes were best in class, putting us on the national map for employment social enterprise. But we were turning away hundreds of women from our program due to capacity issues. Because we hired the women we served to work in our food production business, which generated about half our organization's revenue, sales were the leading indicator for how many women we could employ and serve. At the time, we were in a facility we had outgrown. So even if our sales grew significantly, we didn't have the physical space for more employees. Turning away women created a sense of urgency for us all. But growth without a focus on quality of services and outcomes was a compromise we were not willing to make.

Collectively, we began making reference to how we might serve more women and serve them better. This rallying cry was powerful because every member of the team could see how it applied to them. They set goals for themselves individually and within their departments. In internal staff meetings, at board meetings, and in our external communications, frequent reference was made to serving more women better. It served as a raison d'être for our collective action and helped us move to the next level organizationally—and served us well as the COVID pandemic hit in 2020. We were able to respond to the increased demand for our products as well as the growing needs of the women we served and launch a capital campaign to help us move to a new facility and address our capacity issues.

The leader worth following must build a supportable vision that is both grounded in the present and focused on a desirable future state that followers feel invested in. The vision must be ambitious and appropriately groundbreaking for the organization's current state while being cognizant of the starting point. Being part of a mission-driven nonprofit like WBP is not a requirement for creating an inspiring vision, but a collective understanding of why the organization exists is necessary. Why the team members matter to the larger purpose of the organization is essential. Armed with a compelling vision, a leader worth following can help their team members feel inspired.

Then there are leaders who create a vision so grand they give their followers space to become better than they ever imagined—

even to the point of changing the world. A visionary leader understands how audacious a vision can be for the organization they lead. They also balance the audacity with asking themselves what kind of vision would endure beyond their time as the leader. A visionary leader plays the long game, and the vision must push against what the followers believe is currently possible.

Followers don't get excited about incremental or small changes, so the vision should be aspirational. When President John F. Kennedy announced the mission to go to the moon, it wasn't certain America would succeed. But Kennedy believed the country had the wherewithal to achieve the goal of sending a man to the moon and returning him safely to Earth.

The statement of the goal began with Kennedy's confidence in the ability of Americans to excel, as reflected in his speech given at Rice University in September 1962:

"We choose to go to the moon in this decade and do the other things, not because they are easy, but because they are hard, because that goal will serve to organize and measure the best of our energies and skills, because that challenge is one that we are willing to accept, one we are unwilling to postpone, and one which we intend to win…"[12]

Wow, talk about a grand vision. President Kennedy's ask of the American people and Congress contained a specific date: before the end of the decade. It could be visualized: a man to the moon and back. It was a grand idea: going to the moon! And while it was impossible at the time the president laid out his vision, he acknowledged that fact and said that the difficulty of the goal was the reason to do it. This grand dream created a rallying cry for

Americans and the commitment to the vision led to an amazing accomplishment. Though President Kennedy didn't live to see it happen, two American astronauts walked on the moon only seven years later. This illustrates what becomes possible when a leader creates a vision that inspires others to become part of its realization.

Kennedy certainly had an advantage. He was an elected leader. He was charismatic and led during a time of optimism for the country. Kennedy knew his audience. He had scanned the environment and understood what the country's current capabilities were but was also able to articulate a goal that was so large and audacious it had the power to rally the American people and Congress to provide the support and resources to make it a reality.

Not all visions are moonshots. While it can be overwhelming to sift through the plethora of input from the environment, leaders worth following have the ability to find balance between their own values and the values of the organization to create a vision that will inspire others. Being passionate about the company's work is not enough. The leader must create the vision in response to a compelling problem to solve or an opportunity that must not be missed. The overarching purpose driving the vision must be clear to those who are being asked to follow and to contribute to its success. Then the vision provides the purpose—a compass for everyone involved.

Enlisting others to join the leader in working toward accomplishing the vision is the next lesson. Ready?

Chapter 4
Be the Proselytizer of the Dream

With the vision clearly defined, it's time to enlist people to join the leader on the quest to realize it. A leader's most essential and satisfying moment is when it becomes clear that others buy into the vision. If the vision is developed in an iterative fashion with input from the team (which you learned about in the last chapter), it will be an articulation of what everyone has already realized is the best and most bold direction for the organization. When presented in a way that is both compelling and appealing, it enlists people who want to serve the vision because the dream is larger than any one individual.

In 2023 I was leading the Bean Project through the next strategic planning process. The plan introduced in 2018 had culminated in 2022 with the move to a new facility that was twice the size of the previous building and infinitely better in so many ways. Because of the pandemic, we didn't move directly into a new strategic plan. Instead, we took the time to assess how the needs of the women we served had changed because the community had shifted dramatically as a result of COVID. For the majority of 2020 to 2023, we were hiring and serving women who were in greater crisis than we had ever seen. Nearly all the women we hired were experiencing housing instability or homelessness and had recent and tenuous sobriety or were experiencing debilitating mental health challenges. Their struggles to survive superseded their ability to go to work every day. While the human services team members within our organization worked hard to support the program participants as best they could, for many of the women we employed, keeping a job was an insurmountable struggle. During this time, we reached a point at which 77 percent of the women who did not complete the program failed because of relapse.

We knew we couldn't continue to offer services that were proving ineffective and expect different results. We regrouped and discussed in depth the characteristics of women we were best suited to serve. Like peeling back the layers of an onion, we questioned everything, including the structure of the job, the support services we offered, and how we were measuring success. Serving more women better continued to drive our thinking, but now we needed to reconsider who was included in the "more" and what did "better" really mean. In 2022, the move to the new facility created space to grow our business, hire more women, and expand the program services we could offer. However, I felt strongly that the building was just concrete, bricks, and mortar until we made it into something that served the community.

The conversations around updating the vision took place over nine months. During that time, we didn't stand still but instead began implementing changes based on the information we were gathering. Before we could update our vision, we knew we needed to understand more about the needs of the women in our community and to consider who we were best suited to serve. We refined the tools for measuring our outcomes and identified six areas of self-sufficiency the women were most struggling with, realizing that if we did not address those six things, women wouldn't be able to complete the program. The Big Six, as we called them, focused our team and gave us a concrete way to measure changes in our impact. Though this work made the process of updating the vision longer, it was essential for us to get grounded in our present reality.

In the meantime, we also began using our new facility to offer more services for people we did not employ. A mobile food pantry came to our parking lot twice a month to offer food to our program participants, along with other community members. Before we hired each cohort, we invited all qualified applicants to come for a group interview day during which they could connect with other resources in the community, such as housing or sobriety support, regardless of whether or not they were hired. We partnered with an organization that provided gently used baby and toddler supplies and encouraged Women's Bean Project program participants to use our account to order enough supplies to share with extended family members. The program participants felt proud that they were not only bringing home a paycheck but were able to bring additional resources to their extended family members. Our reach was expanding even while we were continuously improving on our core work.

I could see how proud our team felt when they saw the line at the food pantry truck or when forty women showed up for a group interview and received support, even though we were only hiring about a dozen of the women who came to the group interview. I realized the potential impact WBP could have if we expanded our thinking beyond hiring women to work in our food production business and only providing the employees with support services. What if we thought differently and aimed to impact more lives? What came out of the strategic planning was an overarching vision to impact two thousand lives during the course of the three-year plan. At that time, we were hiring about sixty women each year, so this goal represented significantly greater reach into the community.

Immediately after adopting the new strategic plan with the vision of impacting two thousand lives, the team started referring to how many people beyond the women we hired were impacted by the services we offered. As the leader, this was one of my favorite parts of the process because this was when the vision moved beyond *me* and became one that belonged to *us*. Through the years, the vision that was developed during the strategic planning process has been repeated back to me over and over again as our team, clear on the what, figures out the how.

The leader must be the first person to become adept at articulating the vision, so everyone understands why the work leads to achieving the desired future state. When the dream is sold well, it creates purpose within the team. The leader who effectively paints the picture of the preferred future and helps followers see a part of themselves or their input reflected in the vision makes it more likely followers will join them. The bigger the vision, the bigger the motivation to follow.

In this role of selling the dream, the leader must find the balance between complacency—why should we change, everything is fine right now—and urgency, while avoiding a level of urgency that makes the team anxious. The idea that everything is urgent or conversely that lack of change will lead to certain doom is demotivating and leaves followers feeling anxious and fearful. This can lead to a lot of activity without movement toward the vision as well as burnout and, ultimately, a climate that resists change. For followers to care about the vision, they need to know what is in it for them and why they should care, as well as why action toward realizing the vision is better than inaction or becoming complacent. Setting a vision that is time-bound helps to create enough urgency to provide motivation. Then, the leader paints a picture of the better future and why it matters.

When the leader says to their followers, "Hey, everyone! Come with me on this journey to a brighter future. I don't know exactly how we will get there, but I am confident we have what it takes to reach our vision together," followers then have the privilege of determining how the vision will be pursued. Communicating openness to working together doesn't show weakness or incompetence. The leader's role is to imbue followers with the confidence that they have what it takes to realize the vision if they all believe in it.

But even when the vision is developed with collective input, there may still be team members who have not bought in and don't want to join. A well-articulated vision also allows people to opt out. The leader must then bless and release them. While there is space to discuss and debate how to accomplish the vision, a follower's lack of alignment to the vision is not tolerable and is unhelpful to the rest of the team. Loyalty and retention are built when the team is aligned.

Ford's revolutionary vision

Any research on visionary leaders is likely to yield information about Henry Ford, who is well-known for his namesake company, Ford Motor Company. However, people may not realize that Ford's vision was not about making automobiles. His vision was to bring mobility to all people by making automobile ownership affordable for everyone. He believed mobility would change the way people lived. To realize his vision, he had to find a way to make autos in a cost-effective way and motivate the workers at his company to join him.

Ford believed mass production was the way to realize this vision. Yet, in the early twentieth century, workers had no reason to care about the vision of their company's owner. Imagine being a factory worker during the Industrial Revolution. In the early morning you headed to the factory, often with other family members, including your children. You entered the factory, filled with unsafe conditions such as fumes, dust, and debris, and operated huge equipment with few safety mechanisms. After fourteen to sixteen hours with only two breaks, you went home to sleep for a few hours before you returned to do it all over again, six days a week, for a total of about one hundred hours each week. Not surprisingly, these conditions led to high turnover of employees—at one point reaching about 380 percent for Ford Motor Company.

Ford must have realized he would not reach his vision of mobility for all unless he incentivized his workers to participate in making automobiles more efficiently. In 1914, Ford Motor Company was one of the first companies to cut the workday to eight hours and the number of days worked each week to five. Ford also introduced a $5.00-per-day pay standard (up from $2.50 per day). The implementation of production lines decreased the time to make an automobile from twelve hours to three, lowering the cost of the cars. The combination of better working conditions, higher pay, and lower cost allowed workers to be able to buy the automobiles they built. In fact, the cars were so accessible, ten thousand workers signed up to buy automobiles on the first day they were available. Such adoptions indicate the workers' eventual buy-in to the vision, even if they wouldn't have initially imagined themselves capable of caring about it.

Looking back at Ford's success, it might appear to have been easy. He improved his workers' lives at a time when such action was an anomaly. As he was implementing the changes, he likely faced resistance, particularly from other factory owners. After all,

Ford's actions changed the standards for workers. Change is hard, even when staying the same is undesirable, because status quo is comfortable. At least followers know what to expect. As the leader enlists people to join them in realizing the future vision, the leader must understand their role as the promoter of the change.

Change leadership

When we speak about the leader being responsible for a vision and enlisting others to buy into it, we are referring to change leadership. By definition, change leadership is about transformation, the kind that moves organizations to accomplish things that make the world different, or at least buck the status quo. Great visions are about creating disruption and not settling for incremental change. People are not inspired by small change. Grand visions have the potential to create urgency because the world will be so much better if the vision is realized. Great visions are about big leaps, and big leaps require change leadership.

A change leader develops the vision, motivation, and processes to make change possible. While the leader is selling the dream and getting followers excited about the vision for a better future, they must emphasize a focus on improvement and adaptability and why the changes being made are the path to realizing the vision. Change leadership doesn't come naturally or easily to many. The inclination to manage rather than lead is strong.

Management consultant John Kotter has written extensively about change leadership. As Kotter explains it, change management is a set of tools, processes, and mechanisms designed to ensure that, when changes are made, the team plays along with the changes. Change management is about driving change while keeping the processes controlled and the project on budget. It's better for small changes rather than transformational change.

By contrast, Kotter says, change leadership is about going after big dreams with a sense of urgency. As the leader worth following is enlisting people to join them in their pursuit of the vision, they are also setting the stage for holding the followers accountable for their role in pursuing the company's vision rather than focusing on controlling their followers. Once the vision is agreed on, the team must share the responsibility for working toward it. This means the team must measure, monitor, and manage the correct metrics so they know where they stand and where they are headed, but every action must be connected to the higher purpose, and the team must be given feedback showing that they are moving in the right direction.[13]

To care about the vision, followers must know what's in it for them and why they should care. For Ford's employees, this meant more money with fewer hours and earnings that could lead to their own family's mobility.

Henry Ford's vision was that mobility would change the way people lived. By making automobile ownership affordable for all, he brought mobility to many more people. That was the what. He then focused on the how, which involved making automobiles in a cost-effective way. As the owner, Ford had the power to change the workers' pay and working conditions, but he couldn't accomplish the rest of his vision alone. He had to enlist the workers at Ford Motor Company to join him in realizing the vision. By incentivizing workers who otherwise had few protections in the early twentieth century, Ford was able to realize the vision. Was it self-serving? Yes, but for a leader to realize any vision, they must sell the dream and make it worthwhile for the followers, then lead the change.

While the leader's job is to articulate the vision and the future state it will create and mobilize the needed resources to jump-start the team to implement change, being the proselytizer of the dream is a continuous process. Yet, as you continue to sell the dream, you'll encounter resistance from a variety of sources and for a wide range of reasons. To stay on track, you'll need to learn how to keep your eye on the prize. The next lesson will highlight how to stay on track, even in the face of resistance.

Chapter 5
Keep Your Eye on the Prize

Sometimes getting buy-in isn't the most difficult part of working toward a vision. Instead, staying the course is the bigger challenge. A worthwhile vision requires that the leader keep progressing, even in the face of resistance.

As the leader of the Indian National Congress, Mahatma Gandhi led the Indian struggle for independence from British rule. His vision was to ease poverty, expand women's rights, and achieve self-rule. Though he was often met with violence from the British, Gandhi used fasting and noncooperation as his tools for protest and urged other Indians to do so as well. While not the originator of the principle of nonviolence, Gandhi was the first to apply it on a large scale in the political realm. Gandhi declared that British rule of India was only possible because Indians cooperated with the British. If Indians refused to cooperate, British rule would collapse.

By focusing on a vision for independence through noncooperation, Gandhi consistently requested that his fellow

Indians express their frustrations peacefully and by boycotting British goods and services, such as burning the British clothing they owned, boycotting British courts of law, or resigning from British employment. He pushed for nonviolence even in the face of violence from the other side. As tensions flared and the British responded with increasingly violent resistance, Indians began meeting violence with violence. Gandhi implored his fellow Indians to stop all violence and cease property destruction. He began a hunger strike to pressure Indians even further and encourage them to instead focus their influence on crippling the British India government economically, politically, and administratively. Through it all, Gandhi kept his eye on the prize. By maintaining the position that the ultimate aim was independence and not getting distracted by the British reaction, Gandhi captured people's imagination and continued to push his idea that they should meet hate with love.

Additionally, he met his fellow Indians on their own turf, traveling across the country to enlist people to join him in the movement for Indian independence. He proposed the idea that Indian civilization could be driven by soul force and morality, a distinct departure from the brute force and immorality he accused Western cultures of.

When the British finally decided to negotiate, their strategy was to divide the Indian people by religion and caste, appealing separately to Hindus, Muslims, and those in the lowest caste, considered untouchables. But again, Gandhi kept his eye on the prize of independence for the country. He was concerned the British strategy would divert attention from the goal of independence and lead to divisiveness that would remove the Indians from the goal of ending colonial rule. He insisted the Indian people continue to work together in their efforts of noncooperation.

India gained independence from British rule in August 1947, but Gandhi only saw it for a few months before he was assassinated in January 1948. October 2, Gandhi's birthday, is now known as the International Day of Non-Violence. He maintained the stance that moral power gained through nonviolence would prevail over physical power through violence.[14]

By creating an example of nonviolence in the face of resistance, Gandhi made possible the changes necessary to achieving the vision of Indian independence. Gandhi also set the stage for future leaders such as Dr. Martin Luther King Jr. to use civil disobedience and nonviolent protests to advance the civil rights movement in America.

Levels of resistance

Of course, not all leaders of change face such violence. Generally, the people who seem to like change are the ones who are implementing it, while those who feel as though the change is being done *to* them tend to resist. And while resistance in the business world is not usually violent, research from author Rick Maurer found that, more often than not, leaders implementing change in organizations confront resistance in ways that manifest as apathy, inertia, or opposition.[15]

In the first level of resistance that followers experience, the leader might hear things like "I don't get it." This can happen because the followers don't believe they have enough information about why the change is being implemented, they disagree with the data being used to justify the change, or they are confused about the meaning of the information provided. Leaders who receive this type of resistance typically respond with more information to clarify their position. However, too often, leaders treat all resistance to change as level one resistance, believing that if only they continue to bombard followers with information, they will get their buy-in.

Level two resistance is about followers not liking the change. This happens when the followers have an emotional reaction to change based on fear. The reasons underlying the fear can be that the followers think they will lose control, their job, their status, or their pride—think of times when change involves structural revisions to the organization, work or job reassignments, or layoffs. Even the followers who remain or whose position isn't changed can struggle. Too often, the leader defaults to continuing to provide information about why the change is necessary, how the change will improve the company, or other pieces of information to justify the change. Whether true or not, once followers have an emotional response to change, they stop listening to information and have a hard time controlling their further responses.

In the third level of change resistance, followers' feelings shift to negativity about the leader and opposition to the proposed changes. Maybe it's because the followers don't like the leader or because the way the change is being implemented has eroded their trust or confidence in the leader. At this level, resistance becomes focused on the leader, not the change itself.

Followers don't live on each level separately. All three can come into play at the same time. People resist change for a variety of reasons. Followers perform their work based on an agreement they feel they have with their leader, and change can challenge these agreements. Or they don't like how the change is being implemented. They might also be afraid of what their job will look like once change happens. A leader, while keeping their eye on the vision they are seeking to move the organization toward, must also identify where the resistance lies and how to address it effectively.

Level one resistance can be overcome with information about why the changes are being made, what is happening, and how the changes will be implemented. For level two resistance, the focus should be more on the followers, addressing their fears and talking about what's in it for them. This is an opportunity to talk about how the change will make the followers' situations better or to be honest about whether the change could harm them or their positions. Level three resistance must be overcome by working on the relationship between the leader and their followers. Leaders must focus on building trust by doing what they say they will and admitting if mistakes are made.

After leaders clearly articulate the vision and enlist others to join them in the work toward realizing the vision, they must ensure they aren't distracted by the messiness of people's opinions and concerns that surface while working to make progress. Leaders must ask questions to be sure they truly understand the reasons for resistance, because followers may be sharing helpful information that will inform the strategy and increase the likelihood of success, rather than merely creating obstacles.

But if the leader is not fully committed to their vision, it can be easy to change course in the face of resistance. Keeping their eye on the prize means the leader is incorporating helpful input and addressing any resistance while they continue to sell the dream of a better future. Followers want to know the leader is committed to the vision. After all, if the leader wavers from their commitment, how can followers be expected to stay committed?

Visions shouldn't stagnate

Keeping one's eye on the prize doesn't mean ignoring the changing environment. Every leader should stay aware of outside influences that make implementing the vision a challenge. The leader must constantly gather input from followers, the marketplace reaction to change, and the results as they come in, continually updating the vision based on this input.

As the automobile market grew, customers began exerting their power and requesting automobiles in different colors. Ford famously said, "Any customer can have a car painted in any color that he wants so long as it is black."[16] By this time, Ford had begun to realize his vision of mobility for all—to the point where consumers had become more discerning. Ford's unwillingness to update his vision and incorporate the wishes of customers was a misstep and led to a drop in market share for Ford Motor Company.

As the leader brings people along in realizing the vision, there will undoubtedly be challenges and resistance. Invariably, the world will change while the team is working on changing the world. In the face of these challenges, the leader must be in tune with their followers' feedback and the shifts happening around them. They will need to continue to connect the dots and address everyone's concerns. As a vision is pursued, leaders will have multiple moments when they have to adapt while also staying as true as possible to the original vision of a better future. Staying the course despite resistance is the hardest part of leading change.

Gandhi was met with resistance from all sides as he worked toward his vision for Indian independence. He believed the Indian people would be better off without British rule, even if the path to getting there would be difficult and his fellow countrymen weren't initially inclined to follow him. Even the most optimistic leaders can feel discouraged. Yet, the most impactful leaders are those who keep their focus on the vision because they believe so strongly in it and who keep hope in the vision alive, for themselves and their team.

Chapter 6
Be a Hopeslinger

In the Old West, the reputation of gunslingers was that they used the most powerful weapons of the time to enforce the law, as well as to wreak havoc in towns across the western US and territories. They were known to be quick on the draw and to prevail in a gunfight. Today, the most impactful leaders use hope as one of the most powerful weapons of our time to inspire followers to join them in pursuit of a vision.

Napoleon Bonaparte is often quoted as having said, "A leader is a dealer in hope."[17] A leader's responsibility is to offer followers a vision and direction that inspires and generates hope as a way to motivate them. After selling the vision to the team and overcoming resistance to change, hope becomes the most important tool in helping the team realize the vision. To be hopeful, followers must feel the vision is possible to attain. This is about building a sense of possibility, not just wishful thinking. By creating a true belief that something better is possible, the leader is dealing in hope.

In his "I Have a Dream" speech, Dr. Martin Luther King Jr. invited others to join him in envisioning an America in which all people enjoyed the benefits of equality and belonging. Dr. King's gift was his ability to craft a narrative of a future that was different, better, and, in his words, promised to the people. In his speech during the March on Washington in 1963, he spoke about collecting on the promissory note created by America's founders in the Declaration of Independence and the Constitution: that all men are created equal and guaranteed certain inalienable rights of life, liberty, and the pursuit of happiness. King told the marchers they were there to collect on this defaulted promissory note.[18] Metaphorically, this speech created a promise of a better future the audience could rally behind. King was slinging hope to his audience.

Dr. King's ability to inspire hope was founded in his ability to relate to the people he was leading. When he spoke about a dream for his own children, that one day they would be judged by the content of their character rather than the color of their skin, he put forth a dream any parent could understand and be motivated to pursue. Many of King's speeches during the civil rights movement were instrumental in generating hope for a better future for millions of people.

Hope is not generated through an ethereal vision but from tangible, time-bound goals. King's statement, "We must accept finite disappointment, but never lose infinite hope,"[19] illustrates this concept. Hope is energy to which we all have access. If leaders can help followers tap this infinite source, anything is possible. Hope motivates people to move beyond their perceived limitations because they can imagine something better. In the same way Dr. King shared his dream of a new future for an America with equality for all, every leader is creating some form of a dream for a better future when they are selling their vision. The March was a demonstration showing support of a vision that was bigger than any one individual present, and King spoke about the dream in terms followers could imagine realizing, giving them hope and drive.

Positive energizers

Kim Cameron, cofounder of the University of Michigan's Center for Positive Organizations, has done research to show how the positive relational energy created by some leaders' behaviors results in extraordinary outcomes. Relational energy can be described as the positive feelings and sense of increased resourcefulness people experience as a direct result of an interaction with someone else.[20] Some leaders are able to increase the energy of those around them as well as their feelings of positivity. They exchange energy in a way that helps followers feel lifted up and enthused. This positive energy is contagious and creates feelings of hope among followers. Cameron refers to leaders who are able to lift up groups as positive energizers.

Positive energizers uplift others because they demonstrate and cultivate virtuous actions like humility, compassion, and kindness. Their displays of trust, honesty, and generosity help everyone in the organization flourish. The notion of lifting up others has become even more important in these post-pandemic, media-heavy times. Leaders who are positive energizers have a distinct advantage because the ability to use this energy is a predictor of leadership and organizational success. Followers of positive energizers display higher levels of engagement, have lower turnover, and experience greater feelings of well-being.[21]

For positive energy to exist, leaders must be rooted in hope because generating hope within others is key to realizing any vision for the future. This hope helps leaders see potential all around them—in difficult situations, in their followers, and in their own ability to lead through challenges. The leader worth following is the lead hopeslinger, and their positive energetic behaviors such as resilience, forgiveness, and kindness create hope in their followers.

Hope and resilience

The condition of having hope is also linked to improved resilience. Women's Bean Project used a survey tool called the Employment Hope Scale to measure program participants' feelings of hope around their employment prospects because hope leads to improved feelings of self-efficacy and the ability to stick with a task even when it becomes challenging.

At the beginning of each program cohort's tenure, I had the opportunity to sit with them and introduce myself. I encouraged them to create a vision for what they wanted their futures to look like when they completed the WBP program and beyond. I suggested that with this grounding of a vision for their futures, they could then go to work each day and take actions that got them closer to the lives they wished to have. During this conversation, I emphasized that the Bean Project was more concerned with their futures than their pasts. I reminded them that the past didn't define them, but that the opportunity within their grasp in the upcoming six to nine months could define their futures. WBP's commitment was to provide the resources and teach the skills to place the tools in their employment toolbox. What they did with the opportunity was up to them. My aim in having this conversation with the women was to plant seeds of hope that would sprout throughout their time at WBP. I wanted them to dream of what they wanted to create for their lives, instill hope in them that the dream was possible, and then promise we would all be there for them as they worked toward their dreams. The interesting thing about the Employment Hope Scale results was that, over time, we realized they were skewed. By virtue of being hired at the Bean Project, women felt more hopeful. We eventually stopped using the tool and instead focused our efforts on harnessing that hope we knew they felt throughout the remainder of their tenure with us.

Research shows that in order to set goals, one must be hopeful. Since goal setting and working toward those goals was an integral part of the Bean Project's program, measuring hope served as an indicator of each woman's ability to work toward her goals. To be clear, hope is not optimism. Optimism is a belief that good things will happen. Hope is the will and determination to move ahead despite what is happening. It's about agency. Hope fuels the goals set by the women at the Bean Project because it's the belief that things can be made better with one's actions. For followers, hope can motivate the team to work harder and face the odds with an attitude that, through the team's actions, they can be successful.

Researcher Kaye A. Herth has explored the connection between leadership and hope. In Herth's terms, hope is an active expectation of a better tomorrow. It helps to create the flexibility and adaptability to survive changing environments and allows one to move forward with a confident expectation of achieving what they are working toward. A hopeful person feels the expectation of a brighter future.

When leaders lead from a hope perspective, it allows them to show their authenticity, courage, and purpose. This perspective proves effective in times of rapid change and situations that create uncertainty. Leading with hope influences decision-making because it requires taking appropriate action at the right time with the expectation of a positive outcome. A hopeful leader catapults themself and others into a future that is better.[22]

Throughout history, leaders have demonstrated that their ability to lead through challenges can be attributed to their ability to generate hope in others. Leading from a hope paradigm involves being hopeful and having a hopeful vision while also minimizing things that inhibit hope, such as low energy, reactions to uncontrollable pain and suffering, multiple losses, and the devaluation of people. Instead, the leader must create an environment that fosters creativity and openness to new ways of doing things, giving everyone space to express their ideas. Being lighthearted can help foster hope. It may also allow you to gain perspective, be more flexible toward change, and increase your ability to balance competing interests.

Abundance versus scarcity

I believe a focus on hope leads to a mentality of abundance. I am a much better leader when I approach each situation from a place of abundance rather than scarcity. Too often, companies default to a scarcity mindset—especially NGOs. They perceive that they are competing with one another for funding, and they hold their processes and systems close to the vest to prevent others from copying them. They focus on what they don't have over what they have, what they cannot do over what they can, and on the problems rather than hope-filled solutions. This is a shame because no single organization or company will be able to change the world. It will take all of us, working together to overcome society's most intractable problems.

When we instead view the world with the belief that everyone has something to offer and, in fact, everyone is already offering something, we leave room for hope. The leader's job is then to figure out what followers are offering that will help them accomplish the vision or coach them to offer what is needed. By approaching each situation and person from a place of abundance, the leader can determine what is needed from the team to become successful.

Hope is the leader's most effective tool in enlisting people to join them in realizing the vision. How does the leader inspire hope? Dr. King did it with his oratorical abilities, but a leader worth following can inspire people to dream more, learn more, do more, and become more by being a hopeslinger—a leader who uses hope as their most powerful tool.

Now that you know the importance of vision and the lessons of dot connection, selling the dream, keeping your eye on the prize, and being a hopeslinger, it's time to move to the next characteristic a leader worth following must display: integrity.

Chapter 7

Integrity

In December 2023, Spotify CEO Daniel Ek announced layoffs for 17 percent of the Spotify workforce. In a memo announcing the reduction in force, he spoke about the actions he had taken a couple of years earlier when capital was cheap. Ek acknowledged the company had taken advantage of low interest rates and had invested to expand the team, enhance content, and try new initiatives. He went on to say the investments largely worked. Yet the company was still reducing its workforce by 1,500 people. While 1,500 people lost their jobs, Ek kept his.

The disconnect was hard to reconcile. While on the one hand he said the investments worked, on the other he was laying off people who had trusted his leadership. When Ek's actions didn't yield the hoped-for results from the capital infusion, he didn't take responsibility for his role in the failure. It's unclear why, if the activities were successful, the layoffs were necessary, and Ek missed the opportunity to share with his followers his own role in the failed strategies.[23]

Leaders worth following hold themselves to a higher standard, knowing that others will hold them accountable. They learn from their mistakes and don't blame others or fail to take responsibility for their actions. A key aspect of leadership includes being accountable to one's followers. It's hypocritical to hold others accountable if the leader isn't doing the same for themself. Without accountability and a willingness to take responsibility, there is no integrity. Without integrity, the leader has no authority to lead.

Warren Buffet defines integrity as operating from an honesty mindset, embracing change, and rejecting wrongdoing. In Buffet's view, three things are important in the people he hires: intelligence, initiative, and integrity. And, as Buffet says, if integrity is not present, hopefully the person is "dumb and lazy," because without integrity, intelligence and initiative can be misguided or even harmful. Being ethical and honest outweigh intelligence.[24]

Honest, trustworthy, reliable. These are the building blocks of integrity. How a leader behaves with small ethical challenges sets the stage for how they will handle big issues. Having integrity builds trust with followers because they don't have to worry about the motives behind the leader's actions, saving a lot of the time and emotional energy needed for interpretation. The followers know they can take the leader at their word.

Honesty in the face of hardship

Being honest even when it is hard is essential. I recall a time early in my tenure at the Bean Project when I struggled with this. I had inherited several staff members who, because of the financial crisis the Bean Project had been going through prior to my arrival, had experienced collective workplace trauma as they watched the board of directors ask several of their coworkers and their former leader to leave. I felt the best action I could start with was listening, so I scheduled one-on-one meetings with each of the four remaining staff members. My second meeting was with Jaci, who, when I asked how long she had been with Women's Bean Project, said, "Eighteen months, and I've spent the last nine months feeling anger and resentment." Clearly, I had work to do to build trust with her and the rest of the team. Everyone was watching closely to see what I would do. After several months of listening to all constituents, from staff to board members, volunteers to donors, I made some decisions about the positions that would best serve the organization at that time.

One of those decisions was to change Jaci's job. After our initial meeting on my first day during which she had shared her frustrations, Jaci's attitude improved. However, six months into my tenure, her attitude had begun to sour again, and the resentment was returning with a vengeance. I wasn't sure how I could lead the team with such a negative presence, and I wasn't confident that Jaci was the right person to keep on the team. But rather than address this directly, I decided to change the responsibilities of her position to those I knew she wasn't qualified for. I informed her that her job was changing and she was welcome to apply for the new position that included some of her old responsibilities as well as many new ones. I shared that we would open the application process to other candidates as well. Upon being told she could apply for the updated position, Jaci's attitude devolved even further into outward anger. Our final conversation ended with her resigning followed by me asking her to leave immediately.

Even today, twenty years later, I cringe to think of what a cowardly move that was. The trust I had worked for months to build with the entire team was gone in an instant. Rather than address Jaci's attitude problems directly, I chose an indirect and dishonest way of dealing with it. I had to start again in building trust with the team members who remained. I learned my lesson and have never done anything like that since.

A leader worth following can be trusted to be honest even when it is hard to be. They have the integrity to say what they mean. They recognize that their followers are listening to more than the words they use and are watching what they do as well. Leaders with integrity lead by example, openly and honestly doing the right thing, treating others with respect, and behaving in a way that clearly shows what they stand for and value. When leaders behave in these ways, followers know they can rely on them.

Has there been a time when you could have been more honest in your interactions with others? How might you behave differently in the future?

Going high

Michelle Obama provided a great example of integrity when she spoke at the 2016 Democratic National Convention. After eight years of serving as the First Lady of the United States, she used her platform to speak about how she and her husband urge their daughters to ignore questions about their father's citizenship or faith and to recognize that the hateful language they might hear from public figures doesn't represent the true spirit of America. Though speaking in the context of what she and her husband tell their children, she was also speaking as a leader to people everywhere, explaining that when someone is cruel or acts like a bully, it's best not to stoop to their level. Instead, she said, "When they go low, we go high."[25]

The mantra "when they go low, we go high" has stayed with me as it has provided me with words for a core belief I have: Always take the high road. I've learned there is no need for me to point out when another person is being unkind or unethical. It will eventually become apparent to everyone. In the meantime, I must stick to what I believe is right.

Leaders who take the high road don't allow themselves to be brought to the level of those who criticize or slander them, even when it's tempting to respond directly. Though President Lincoln's beliefs were firmly antislavery, his motivation for signing the Emancipation Proclamation was, as he said, "to save the Union, and it is not either to save or to destroy slavery." The president hoped that freeing the slaves would lead formerly enslaved people to join the Union army or otherwise help the cause.[26]

Despite being harshly criticized for signing the Emancipation Proclamation, President Lincoln stayed true to his beliefs that it was right and moral to end the institution of slavery, while also fulfilling his responsibility to the country by trying to keep it together. The connection between his ethical beliefs and his moral action—doing what he believed was right and continuing to follow through despite grave opposition—are what made President Lincoln a leader worth following. Lincoln's views opposing slavery weren't merely rhetoric developed during his campaign for the presidency, but always a part of his belief system.[27] His moral convictions continued, even when his desire to free slaves led him to live outside the mainstream views of his time. Lincoln pursued an agenda that alienated many Americans and led the country further into the Civil War, which might have cowed other leaders, but his persistence in pursuing his moral principles was a testament to his leadership.

Bridging the trust gap

We have reached an age in which we have very little trust in, and a lot of cynicism about, leadership. During this time of spin and media interference around our interpretation of the world, it's hardly a wonder that collectively we approach leaders with skepticism. Integrity is even more important to demonstrate today because leaders have a steeper hill to climb to elicit trust. Leaders worth following demonstrate the integrity to bridge the trust gap by realizing their words matter, understanding that leadership isn't about them, and doing what they say they will. They know they will receive the same level of trust they give.

The first lesson of integrity is to realize the weight of your words.

Chapter 8

Realize the Weight of Your Words

As a leader moves into increasingly more senior positions, their words hold more weight. When the leader speaks, followers listen more carefully and respond according to what they believe they hear. A leader's words have the power to break down, confuse, or demoralize followers. Or, a leader's words can build their followers up, making them feel invincible and able to accomplish any vision set before them. Words from leaders inform, persuade, and amplify the beliefs and actions of followers.

Some of the most damaging moments in a person's career can happen because of something a leader says. Years before I became the CEO of Women's Bean Project, I worked as the marketing director for a trade school. I was the only marketing person in the organization and my job was to support the sales team by generating leads the salespeople would eventually convert to school enrollments. The school was owned by two men who met at Harvard Business School. One of the owners took responsibility for overseeing sales and marketing for the school and held weekly meetings with me and the sales team.

Theoretically, this weekly time together made sense; it was a chance to regroup, see what tactics were working, and track progress toward our goals. But the owner didn't conduct the meeting as a productive check-in. Instead, it became a time when individual team members were disparaged. If questions weren't answered quickly enough or to the owner's satisfaction, he would sigh and indicate his displeasure with an eye roll, or he would slam his fist on the table and ask what was wrong with the individual who had garnered his disdain. I vividly recall preparing for these meetings by trying to bring all the materials to answer any question he might possibly ask me.

As we sat around the conference table every Thursday morning, the effect of these meetings became increasingly destructive to the team. Attendees of this weekly meeting actively sought to blame one another to avoid the ire of the owner by withholding information or not speaking up when they were better positioned to provide answers. Outside of these meetings, we seemed to get along well, but once we stepped into the conference room, all bets were off and every person was just looking out for themself.

After many months of these meetings and many sleepless nights from being told I didn't have what it took to do the job, I stopped acting as if I did. This wasn't by choice; I merely lost my confidence about being successful in the job I knew I was qualified for. In the middle of one of the sleepless nights I experienced regularly in those months, I finally decided it was time to stand up for myself. After one of the Thursday meetings, rather than slink back to my desk feeling defeated, I followed the owner out of the room and asked to speak with him. I pleaded with him to stop belittling me in front of my coworkers, pointing out that it damaged our ability to work together. His response was to say, "You know I'm not happy with your work. You have created this problem for yourself." The next day I was fired. Not by the owner, but by another member of senior management.

Though in the long run I bounced back and moved on to new work with renewed confidence, the damage of that leader's words stayed with me for a long time. Reflecting on that experience, I also realized I had learned an important lesson about leadership. Rather than use his words to lift up his team to greater achievements, he used them to degrade. While I believe he understood his words had power, I don't think he understood how to effectively use the power they held to elicit great things from the people he led. He didn't need to be soft or avoid sharing his frustrations. However, he missed the basic tenet that a leader must speak truth for purpose. He could have given honest, open, and timely feedback in a way that was solution-focused and didn't leave his followers feeling less than.

I have learned that before I say something, I must be intentional, asking myself: Is what I am about to say true? Is it kind? Is it useful? Am I using these words with good intention? If the words I am about to say are none of these, I know it's best not to say them at all. Sometimes tough conversations must be had, but before saying things that will be hard for others to hear, it's essential to think about the intention and how to share the message. The leader must always bear in mind that their words carry more weight because of their position. They will never regret giving some thought to the words before speaking them. As Lao Tzu, the Chinese philosopher said, "Watch your thoughts; they become words."[28] Spewing without thinking is dangerous for a leader and their followers.

Inspiring words

Effective language from a leader can motivate, inspire, and foster a sense of purpose. Even the words not directed at followers are important. Despite being harshly judged and disparaged for the Emancipation Proclamation, President Lincoln always treated others with respect and empathy, even when they disagreed with him. Leaders with the ability to take the high road have great power. In his book *Love Your Enemies*, Arthur C. Brooks suggests leaders use words to inspire others with a vision of hope.[29] These leaders know the power of avoiding attacks or insults, even when they disagree. They avoid trying to win arguments or coerce others to come to their points of view. Leaders worth following are ever conscious of their words and their power to lift up or do harm.

Winston Churchill was a leader who understood his words carried weight, and he shaped his speeches with his remarkable command of words. He knew the power of language in communicating effectively and clearly, using simple words without jargon.[30] As he worked to enlist his compatriots to join him in defending Britain from an invasion by Germany, he used facts to make his arguments and incorporated analogies to make complex ideas clear. Churchill was a great orator, using short sentences, key words with repetition, and dramatic pauses to deliver his messages. Churchill was successful at leading because he understood how to represent his ideas in a way followers could grasp and be inspired by.

Adolph Hitler, the dictator of Germany from 1933 until his death in 1945, was also a leader who used words to enlist people to join his Nazi Party agenda. However, he was an irresponsible leader who used uncertainty and fear as tools to motivate his followers. Hitler has been described as a mesmerizing speaker. His words were seductive and manipulative. He gave regular speeches at rallies and on the radio, allowing him to expand his reach into German homes.

When he spoke about his fellow countrymen, he used strong words, and when he spoke about the enemies of the state, he used weak words. His speeches were straightforward and stuck to a single point. As he built the case for Germans to defend themselves, he manipulated them into believing a false dilemma. They could either accept the terms they were presented with at the end of World War I and resign themselves to being second-class citizens, or they could take back their dignity by fighting to regain lost territory.

Hitler was effective because his megalomaniacal visions promised his followers the world. He told Germans who fit the Aryan stereotype they were amazing and he had the answers to their problems. With his words, Hitler labeled people to other them and make them less so they would become more appealing targets for the followers he was enlisting. His followers were seduced by the charismatic vision he laid out at the expense of others. Just as in my experience when my coworkers and I were so relieved when we weren't the target of the owner's vitriol, I suspect many of Hitler's followers were relieved they were not part of the vilified groups.

Both Churchill and Hitler knew words have power to enlist followers. The difference was in how they chose to use the words and their purpose for gaining followers. Both had a vision for their countries for which they used words to convince people to join them in their respective quests. It has been said that while Churchill could convince others *they* could do anything, Hitler was a master at convincing people *he* could do anything. Churchill's approach was direct and concise. He understood the power of repeating strong messages. Hitler was indirect, using euphemisms to disguise actions that would otherwise not be supported.

Kind versus nice

A leader worth following speaks truth for purpose. They don't say things to please others or to look good, but because those things are true. With their words, they stay committed to their core values. They use clear and honest communication and never use their words to tear down or disparage another person. They understand that telling the truth does not have to be cruel.

Leaders worth following understand the difference between being nice and being kind. I believe women leaders are particularly vulnerable to allowing concerns about whether or not they are being perceived as nice affect how they communicate. As a result, they spend a lot of time focused on not hurting feelings and lose authority and respect in the process. They can have trouble getting to the point because they spend so much time worrying about the words they use and dancing around the issues to avoid being seen as mean.

Leaders who are concerned about being nice are focused on how they are being perceived by others. Being kind requires a focus on the other person and using language that is direct and respectful simultaneously. Being kind means the leader provides specific and timely feedback—both positive and negative—that is focused on how the follower feels after they receive it.

Leaders who speak with intention treat situations requiring feedback with the respect the person deserves. They are direct and avoid talking around the subject, even when the situation is uncomfortable. When they give feedback, they talk about observable behavior, how the behavior affects others, and what is expected instead. I have found it's helpful when giving difficult feedback to acknowledge that it may be hard for the other person hear but it is important for their development. Depending on the situation, I might also acknowledge to them that they might not be aware of how they are being perceived or the damage they are doing.

In giving kind feedback, there is space to ask the follower what they would like to do about the problem, while also discussing the consequences if the issue is not addressed. I find ending a difficult conversation with the statement "I am committed to your success" is valuable framing for the person to leave with. I then suggest we follow up on the conversation after an agreed upon period of time to allow the person receiving the feedback a chance to reflect and develop a plan.

Speaking without thinking

I have also learned to avoid randomly ideating aloud. Sometimes I like to say something out loud to see how it sounds. That doesn't mean I believe what I am saying, or that I even agree with it, but rather, I'm trying it on for size. It's a form of verbal processing. I have learned this can be dangerous when my teammates believe they need to act on anything I might say. Even just a simple preface of "I am going to think out loud for a minute" can help mitigate any misunderstanding.

As the leader, it can be challenging to know how your words are being received, so it's important to check in regularly with your team and ask them to share what they heard, as the leader is often the last to know when their words have been misinterpreted.

Have you thought about your words lately? What would you say differently if you were more concerned with being kind than being nice? What ways have your words been misinterpreted? How has that changed the situation?

Words have power, especially when coming from a leader. Leaders must be ever mindful of their words and how they are using them. When persuading others to join the cause and enlisting others in a vision, the leader is required to be in touch with their values and intentions at all times. In this time of a twenty-four-hour news cycle and social media, a leader's words can be amplified in unpredictable ways. Being conscious of the intention and appropriateness of their words serves the leader and their followers, and serves as the foundation for building reciprocal trust.

Chapter 9

Be a Trust Pilot

Employees in high-trust companies feel 74 percent less stress, 106 percent more energy at work, and take fewer sick days.[31] They feel less burnout and take more risks. They express themselves and innovate more. Followers in high-trust environments work better together and produce better outcomes. Amazing things can be accomplished by a team when there is trust. Without it, the team will struggle to share information, take ownership, and collaborate. The stakes are high for a leader to understand how and why trust works and how to build it.

Sometimes leaders forget that trust is reciprocal; they must give trust to get trust in return. Therefore, to build a team, leaders worth following must understand how trust works, how to extend trust to their team members, and then get out of the team's way as they work to accomplish collective goals. It's hard for followers to get inspired by the leader's vision when they don't feel trusted to help pursue it. Without a foundation of mutual trust, they won't believe in the leader's decisions around the direction of the organization or be willing to show up each day ready to advance the mission.

COVID's impact on trust

The lack of reciprocal trust within teams was exposed during the COVID pandemic when suddenly team members were dispersed and required to work from home. As everyone was sent home, leaders who were accustomed to seeing their coworkers in the office found themselves questioning the hours their team members worked. Fearful about losing control over their followers, they used technology to demand online meetings, tracked how quickly team members responded to emails, and showed impatience for the tensions created by the melding of work, home, and school prevalent in most households. You would think this transition to working from home would have been smooth. After all, we had the technology at our fingertips to aid us in the shift to remote work, but we overlooked the social impact—including the stress to our trust relationships—of such radical change in a short period of time. This focus on control eroded trust that might have been present pre-pandemic.

Many leaders misunderstand that trust and control are not the same thing. In fact, the impulse to control impedes the leader's ability to build trust. Having trust means that both parties in a relationship have positive expectations of each other, whereas actions to control send the message there is no faith in one another's intentions.

At the Bean Project, we were forced to create a hybrid work environment during the pandemic. At the onset of the COVID outbreak, our sales began to grow, reaching 45 percent growth by the end of 2020. This helped ensure we were able to keep all our employees, but it also created tremendous pressure to meet the local health and safety requirements for how many people could be on-site at our facility at any given time. At its most restrictive, the mandate was that we allow only 25 percent of our workforce in our building at one time. This required a convoluted shift schedule in which our administrative staff signed up for time slots during each day when they would work in our building. During the rest of the workday, they were expected to work from home.

Though we were able to quickly make the transition to online meetings, I hadn't realized how much I rely on getting the vibe of a person and a situation by watching environmental cues, from subtle facial movements to posture to changes in the other person's tone of voice. Suddenly I was forced into this new online medium to conduct my one-on-one meetings with my teammates, and I felt as though my spidey sense was lost. Rather than worrying about the hours put in by my coworkers, I worried if the trust I had built was created in a way that couldn't be sustained remotely. I adapted by spending much more time during meetings discussing what was going on in this strange new reality presented by the pandemic. Rather than merely sharing the latest mandate about working from home or wearing masks, I told everyone about what I had referenced to come to the decision. I shared what was going on with my kids (both in middle school at the time) with more detail about what was happening at their school than I would have otherwise. Essentially, I was trying to show how we were all being affected by the pandemic and that I was doing my best to bring the latest information to them while also managing personal challenges, just as they were. It was an investment in the personal relationships that would have happened informally when we were all in our building together but was lost when we only saw one another online.

Though it was a challenging time for everyone on at the Bean Project, both personally and at work, we moved from taking for granted that everyone knew their responsibilities and shifted our focus to identifying everyone's roles, defining who was handling what and when, even if those jobs were different from the norm. My aim was to ensure we could leverage the trust we had already built and avoid loss of trust because communication required more intention.

We continued having all-staff meetings that, despite being conducted virtually, were the only time everyone was together. It was a key time for us to connect, maintain, or even build trust with one another. Many of our conversations weren't about work, but instead memories of past holidays or funny stories of our pets' responses to us being home all the time. Focusing on our humanity and interdependence confirmed that we were working toward a purpose larger than just our individual needs and helped us realize we could trust one another, even when we were rarely together face-to-face.

Though the outcomes weren't perfect—we had our share of turnover during the Great Resignation—we were able to emerge from the pandemic restrictions stronger and more resilient. The trust within our team had grown, and we were able to take the elements of our culture that worked well and were solidified during the pandemic into our post-pandemic chapter.

How to build reciprocal trust

It's important to remember that building trust is an incremental process. First, people must know each other. Beyond one another's names, they must know about one another. Where are you from? What are some of your life experiences? Are you married? Do you have kids? What is important to you? What did you do this past weekend? If people show up to work each day and know nothing about one another beyond their current roles, they can only see each other as coworkers and there is no foundation from which to build trust.

From knowing one another and knowing about one another, we begin to realize we like each other. We know we can count on one person to tell good dad jokes (that might be me) and another person will always be a good audience for stories of our kids' antics. When team members like each other, they look forward to going to work each day and spending time together.

When people who work together are able to understand the framing from which they each operate (which is developed through life experience) and they like one another, they can better relate to each other's decisions and feel respect for one another. I worked with a woman who is a single mom of four kids. Though she didn't go to college, she made sure her children did because she understood it would change their future prospects. We have shared stories about raising boys, and I have come to like her very much. Because I know how challenging it is to raise kids in a two-parent household, I have tremendous respect for her and what she has single-handedly helped her children accomplish.

When a relationship is built and respect is achieved, trust can be developed. Trust should be familiar to all of us because it's a feeling that is the same at work as in one's personal life. It's generated from open and honest sharing, consistent communication, and willingness to accept feedback. It requires people to be willing to share who they are, even if it means being vulnerable. This authenticity in relationships allows people to see each other as being on a journey through life and makes space for empathy. When trust is established, team members realize they can count on one another.

Leaders must encourage trust among their team members and build trust with their team collectively and individually. I have a professional friend named Darlene who was named CEO of an organization after the founder left. Darlene had many years of experience in the nonprofit world and felt confident as she took over the role. The organization was at a crossroads when Darlene took the helm. Unlike the Bean Project, they had not prospered during the pandemic and had reached a point where they were not financially stable and needed to consider making changes to their business and revenue model to ensure they survived.

Darlene's confidence in her abilities was evident from the outset. As they mourned the loss of their beloved founder and leader, she walked into the organization with a can-do attitude, ready to identify the problems and fix them quickly. She did analysis, identified what she saw as the most pressing issues, and began implementing changes to their operations at a rapid pace, believing wholeheartedly in everything she did.

I met Darlene when she was a month into the job and the management team that was in place when she arrived was rebelling. She shared stories of some very intense conversations in which one of the team members was particularly disrespectful. She said she pleaded with them to give her feedback but then disagreed with their perspectives when they weren't consistent with her own. She began to believe no matter what she did, they would be unhappy and resist change. She told me she couldn't understand why they were giving her such a hard time and wondered aloud why they couldn't see that what she was doing was the right thing. She was floundering without support from the team. She decided it would be best to fire the disrespectful member of the management team and began to enlist a member of the board to assist her.

Darlene and I spoke several times during those first few months of her tenure with the company. Three months in, she shared she had contracted with her daughter to bring her expertise to the company's business. Darlene felt strongly that her daughter had the right knowledge to help the business get a handle on its cost of goods and operations and give it a chance at a survival.

This may have been true, but for the management team, it was the final straw. Shortly after Darlene told me she brought her daughter in, and four months into her tenure as the CEO, she called me to say she had been fired.

A few months after Darlene's termination, we met for coffee. I was eager to hear how she was doing and provide support because I suspected the firing felt traumatic for someone who had otherwise had a successful career. In broad strokes, she shared some reflections on her time with the organization and the actions she had taken, but I got the distinct impression she wasn't yet ready to look any deeper at how she had contributed to her own demise. Near the end of our conversation, she said, "I just couldn't get them to follow me."

It's certainly easier to watch from the outside and assess another leader's actions and missteps. From my outside perspective, I believe Darlene didn't understand that when she became the CEO, her highest priority should have been to build trust with the team. I suspect the employees who rebelled against Darlene and contributed to her firing never trusted her. Perhaps it was because she didn't understand that the thing that destroys trust faster than anything else is being focused on oneself. Had she invested first in listening and incorporating the team's feedback into her vision, then enlisted the team to join her, she would have had a better chance of success. Though she likely believed hiring her daughter was a good decision, she came across as self-oriented, a surefire way to erode any trust she might have built.

Leaders in trusting relationships

To build and maintain trusting relationships, leaders must be consistent. Followers need to know what they'll get when they interact with the leader. The leader must be reliable—following through and doing what they say they will. They must be approachable and show empathy, focusing on the followers' experience of situations. Leaders must be vulnerable, admitting their own mistakes while also addressing others' errors without diminishing them.

Leaders who build and maintain trust are transparent. They are conscientious about sharing information with their followers so followers aren't left to speculate about what is going on and what the leader intends. Simple language like "here's what I know and what I don't know," "this is what is not true," and "I'm going to learn more about that, and when I do, I will share my understanding with you" shows that the leader trusts their followers, making them more likely to get trust in return.

Of course, sometimes the leader has information that can't be shared. In these instances, they must share what they can and let their team know they will provide more information when they are able. Too often a leader avoids sharing bad news, not because it can't be shared, but because they are afraid to. It's important not to conflate information that can't be shared with bad news. Trust is demonstrated by sharing when it's appropriate, because leaders build trust in part by letting go of control, which includes control of information.

Trust between leaders and followers also includes the balanced distribution of managerial and leadership responsibilities. The leaders avoid second-guessing others, even when the work isn't done the way they would do it. They guide their followers and hold them accountable for the results, not the process. They resist the compulsion to have all the answers for their followers and give them the space to make their own decisions. Being overly involved shows lack of trust.

Followers in a trusting relationship

For their part, followers want to feel the leader is on their side and will treat them fairly. They need to know their opinions matter and are valued and that the leader will have their back and won't compromise their principles to suit the situation, even if it requires an adjustment in thinking. By extending grace, the leader receives grace in return.

In the early days, as he was building his studio and before it became successful, Walt Disney was a participatory leader who ran his studio communally and collaboratively. He recruited hundreds of artists from across the country and offered to educate them to improve their skills. Disney had a knack for sharing his vision and his storytelling techniques with the illustrators. He ensured everyone had a clear role and trusted them to carry the vision forward into their production. With this leadership style, he was able to motivate the artists to create iconic animated films.

As the company grew, Disney's paternalistic style shifted to be more authoritarian. Prior to World War II, as the company became profitable, this style led to many issues with employees who quit or went on strike to show their discontent. After the war, perhaps as he became more mature, Disney's leadership shifted to become more of a guide; he showed his followers trust and they responded. This style kept him out of the details of the company, allowed him to be a mentor and coach, and gave the team the ability to deliver on Disney's vision.[32]

I think of trust between myself and my teammates as a being held in a bank. The account starts out full and, through interactions with one another, we make deposits. Occasionally, trust is breached, and a "tax" is paid. However, I believe just because a tax may potentially be paid, we shouldn't withhold trust out of fear.

Years ago, Scott, our marketing manager, was struggling to get done the work required for the job. I noted his struggle and offered to help him launch the production of our annual catalog. Because we produce the catalog only once each year, we have learned that the timing for distribution is essential to driving our holiday sales. I understood the volume of work required to launch the catalog, having produced others in the past, so I suggested I could help him by getting the project going until he had some other urgent tasks completed. I said I would do the work with his input, but that we couldn't wait until he was ready to get the project started. He bristled at the suggestion and responded with a timeline for producing the catalog that started immediately. So, I backed off.

Weeks later, I asked to check in because Scott hadn't shared any information about progress made, such as design concepts or photography needs, both of which are typical early-stage milestones for the catalog production. Scott and I sat down at the conference table in my office, and he pulled out the timeline, showing what he had done and what was upcoming, reassuring me he was on track. I asked how I could help, and he said he had it under control. Then he went back to his desk, and his supervisor overheard him making a phone call to the designer asking her if she was available to start work on the catalog. Scott had lied. That phone call to the designer was the first step in the catalog production, and only after our meeting did he launch the project.

My husband and I talk with our children about what defines character in difficult situations. Our saying is "It's not what you do. It's what you do about what you did." By this we mean that it's not about your initial mistake, it's about what you do after the mistake is made. Scott had misjudged his ability to get the catalog done, but then when he had the opportunity to accept help, he lied about his progress. I had communicated my willingness to problem solve, assist him, and even take over until he was able to do the work. Instead of admitting he was in over his head, he doubled down on the lie that he was capable.

I called Scott into my office and said, "I know you didn't tell me the truth about what work you have done. I don't think this is who you are, but I do think this is not a job you are capable of doing." We let him go that day. While I was able to give him grace, I was no longer able to trust him. It was time to move on.

Patagonia and trust

Yvon Chouinard, the founder of Patagonia, created a company that has become the leader in sustainable outdoor gear and apparel, as well as a model for corporate transparency. Chouinard always said he never wanted to be a businessman; he was content being a rock climber. He believed a successful business could only be built on a foundation of social and environmental responsibility, so when he created his company to address the needs of rock climbers, he founded it in a way that was values- and purpose-driven, with commitments to environmental sustainability, innovation, and employee empowerment. He believed employees should have autonomy and take responsibility for their jobs. He felt when followers are treated with respect by their leader, they will treat one another with trust and respect.[33]

When Chouinard decided to retire in 2022, instead of passing down the company to the next generation of his family, he changed the ownership by giving the company away. At that time, the company was valued at $3 billion, and the transaction was completed by designing a trust and a nonprofit organization to ensure all the company's profits (about $100 million per year) would be used to combat climate change and protect undeveloped land across the globe.[34] It's remarkable that none of this was done for tax benefits, but because Chouinard believed in what he stood for. The new structure helps to ensure that the trust Chouinard built—with employees and the public—will be carried into perpetuity.

Patagonia, as the company was eventually called, aligned its values with their business objectives by being transparent about their impact on the world. And so far, that trust is holding strong as Patagonia was named the most reputable brand in the US as it celebrated its fiftieth anniversary in 2023.[35]

It all starts with trust

We are living in a paradox: we can be so much more efficient in this high-tech world we are operating in, but the distance technology creates makes it harder to connect. The old paradigm of high-touch, command, and control leadership is out; the new paradigm is about connection. Trust is one of the most important forms of leadership capital.

Have there been times when you have struggled to build trust with your followers? What did you miss? Have you struggled to trust others? Why? What was the outcome?

While building trust is extremely important for the success of the leader and the team, the leader worth following must also recognize it's not all about them, even while others are looking to them for leadership.

Chapter 10
It's Not About You

It can be strange for a new leader to experience others' responses to their change in status. For the first time, all eyes are on them. Their opinions carry more weight. Followers listen closely to what they are saying, reading meaning into their words. Expectations of the leader's performance become higher, and people feel free to criticize, often loudly and publicly, when the leader lets them down. When a leader does well, they can be a hero; when they fail, they can be vilified.

Becoming the CEO of Women's Bean Project was my first role in a nonprofit organization, so I was quite surprised at how many people in the community cared about who was hired to do the job. In the first few months in my role, I met community members who shared that I had been a topic of conversation at their dinner party recently, or they had "heard about me." It was strange to imagine why anyone other than the staff and the board would pay attention to who I was and how I did my job.

Over time, I learned to be mindful of what I said and did. If I responded to a question flippantly, I might be reminded of it at a later date, and often I didn't even recall what I had said. I received calls or emails from people in the community who wanted to know more about decisions to work with certain partners or to discontinue products. I also experienced the heady feeling that came when, based on meeting me, someone would decide to support the Bean Project. When a reporter called, or the local news wanted to do a story, I was the spokesperson for the organization. My name became well-known and, over time, closely associated with WBP.

Because of all the attention I was getting, these experiences gave me my first insight into how a CEO might begin to believe they were the sole key to an organization's success—that it was all about them and their amazing views. Around the time I was taking note of these ego-boosting experiences, Tyco International's CEO, Dennis Kozlowski, was in the news for having received $81 million in unauthorized bonuses, purchasing over $14 million in art, and paying a former Tyco director a $20 million investment banking fee. Under Kozlowski's direction, the company also footed half the cost for a $2 million fortieth birthday party for his wife. He was convicted in 2005 for grand larceny, falsifying business records, securities fraud, and conspiracy. He served more than six and a half years in prison before being released in 2014.

Tyco was very successful during Kozlowski's tenure, and it appeared he was allowed to operate unchecked. He had taken huge liberties with company resources, and the company sued him as well, requiring him to pay back $500 million in compensation and benefits earned during his time of disloyalty to the company. As I read these stories in the news, I remember thinking Kozlowski had made the success of the company about himself. He had fallen into the trap of believing it was all about him. Though my role as a nonprofit CEO barely resembled his, I knew I could never make any of the attention or success about myself—if I did, I would be putting the entire organization in jeopardy.

The pedestal paradox

Despite research showing an increasing lack of trust in leaders, followers frequently find themselves wanting to trust leaders, willing to give them the benefit of the doubt until the leader proves themself unworthy of the trust. Followers want to follow leaders who are worthy of their respect and admiration because being on the same team as a successful leader makes followers feel good about themselves. As the team's success grows, followers often place their leaders on pedestals with their respect and admiration. However, once on the pedestal, expectations shift. Followers expect leaders to be infallible, take big chances, and achieve big wins. They are often willing to forgive or overlook a leader's mistakes in favor of idolization, at least initially.

Leaders are complicit in the pedestal problem. Strong leaders must have confidence their contributions are unique and important. As they experience success, most leaders can't help but feel satisfied with the accolades they receive. And when a leader does something difficult, such as build a company from an idea into a successful business, not only does the leader feel satisfied, but being idolized by their followers can feel like an affirmation to the leader that they are worthy of being on the pedestal. This is commonly seen in the tech world, as founders who create companies worth billions of dollars are revered for their brilliance and begin to believe they can succeed at anything they try.

Followers tend to admire these "unicorns" so much that they remove the leaders from the realm of realistic expectations and accountability. Investors throw money at these leaders for their next big idea, as if they were singularly responsible for the first success. These leaders are seen as invincible, much like a superhero. Part of the charm of superheroes is that they have no insecurities, personal dreams, or aspirations. This dynamic is paradoxical because humans aren't superheroes. They are messy and have emotions and egos.

While followers place leaders on a pedestal, they don't want their leaders to believe they belong there. The pedestal's shine begins to fade when the leader appears to buy into the idea that they can do no wrong and acts as though they really are as brilliant as others have said and things couldn't have been accomplished without them. These "superhero" leaders begin to behave in ways that prove them unworthy of the pedestal, eroding the admiration and trust that got them there in the first place. Once one is on the pedestal, there is nowhere to go but down.

Humbition

When leaders are on the pedestal, followers and leaders are not working together. In this situation, the leader seeks to influence others by wielding status and authority. Humility is an essential quality in managing this dynamic to ensure success doesn't become only about the leader.

The truth is, even the most accomplished people have insecurities that can keep them humble. And though high-profile entrepreneurs may have accomplished things beyond their wildest dreams and aspirations, they must not ever begin to believe their success is singularly attributable to themselves. Instead, leaders worth following must leave themselves room to be human and vulnerable, with a willingness to seek input from others. They must lead in a way that benefits more than just themselves. These leaders must see the spotlight as part of the job and be willing to share the stage with teammates.

Humility is not weakness or timidity and should not be pursued to the exclusion of drive and ambition. Humility and ambition, or humbition, is the combination of confidence, wisdom, and grace. Humbitious leaders acknowledge their own imperfections. As Rick Warren said in his book *The Purpose Driven Life*, "Humility is not thinking less of yourself, it's thinking of yourself less."[36] The leaders worth following realize it's not about them, it's about the people following them.

Saint Mother Teresa referred to humility as the mother of all virtues, saying, "If you are humble, nothing will touch you, neither praise nor disgrace, because you know what you are. If you are blamed, you will not be discouraged. If they call you a saint, you will not put yourself on a pedestal."[37]

Mother Teresa was ambitious, too, devoting her life to helping those with the greatest needs. She founded Missionaries of Charity in India in 1950 and ran the organization for forty-five years. When she died, she was overseeing five hundred missions in one hundred countries. From hospices to homes for people with HIV/AIDS, leprosy, and tuberculosis to soup kitchens, orphanages, and schools, her humbitious focus was to minister to the poor, sick, orphaned, and dying. Yet, despite the ambition needed to grow the scale of her impact, she is also known for her Humility List, a list of fifteen ways to stay humble, including "Speak as little as possible about yourself" and "Do not seek to be admired or loved."

Humility as a key to success

Researchers at the University of North Texas did an analysis of more than two hundred studies and found humble leadership was the strongest predictor of employee satisfaction and strong team and individual performance. Teams led by humble leaders are more likely to share their opinions, take more risks, and produce better quality work.[38] These characteristics, sometimes described as servant leadership, require that the leader's focus be on helping others discover their own power while making the most of team members' skills and talents.

These leaders view the follower's time with the company as part of their professional journey. They acknowledge the follower won't always work in this one company or role and the leader's job is to help the follower develop and get ready for what comes next. These leaders give space for the follower to become the most competent version of themself while modeling what striving to become better looks like. Despite being respected, these leaders avoid the pedestal because they are follower focused.

Don't be a superhero

Leaders worth following are human and let others know it. They find the sweet spot between vulnerability and strength. They leverage their authentic selves to increase the collective effectiveness of the team. They are aware of and manage their own fears and anxieties so they can help others grapple with theirs. They maintain the humility to recognize it's not about them and stay ambitious enough to be a driver of greatness. A leader who allows themself to be placed on a pedestal allows it to be all about them. When this happens, they lose their opportunity to be effective.

How do you balance being in the spotlight and maintaining humility? Are there strategies you've developed to strike this balance? How do you show up in humbitious ways?

A natural progression from realizing the weight of your words and avoiding the pedestal is doing what you say you will, our next lesson.

Chapter 11
Your Word Is Your Bond

When the newest version of ChatGPT came out, it featured a voice called Sky that sounded like the actress Scarlett Johansson. After the updated product introduction, Johansson released a statement saying she had been approached by Sam Altman, CEO of OpenAI, the developer of ChatGPT, asking to hire her to voice the ChatGPT product under development, but she had declined. Nine months later, the new version, ChatGPT-4o came out with a voice that greatly resembled Johansson's.

When confronted about the likeness, Sam Altman said the voice wasn't modeled after the actress and wasn't intended to sound like her. Despite the defense, OpenAI stopped using the voice and apologized for not communicating better. However, it appeared that the problem wasn't poor communication but instead denial of doing something they had been caught doing. That they asked permission to use Johansson's voice, were turned down, and yet seemed to do it anyway represented a huge lapse of integrity. When a leader lies so obviously, it calls into question all the other things they might have lied about that haven't been uncovered yet.[39]

A leader's word is their bond. A leader worth following holds themself to a higher standard for their own accountability than they do others. They do what they say. They are consistent and reliable. They practice what they preach. They keep promises, honor commitments, and, if commitments can't be met, explain why. When mistakes happen, they take responsibility and avoid blaming others.

When a leader worth following holds others accountable, they never embarrass others for their mistakes. They hold conversations about mistakes privately, never using a public forum for such feedback. They are direct, tactful, and respectful with others and give followers the opportunity to behave the same way in return. Too often, leaders avoid having hard conversations, but a leader worth following does not. They allow followers to have a voice in things that affect them and do not retaliate if the message is unwelcome or hard to hear.

Ethical leadership

Ethisphere is an organization that defines and advances the standards of ethical business practices. Each year they recognize companies that demonstrate an unwavering commitment to doing business with ethics and integrity. Companies that make the list show their commitment to operating ethical businesses. Interestingly, these companies also outperform others of similar size.

Ethics matter in leadership and business because they set a clear standard for everyone to see. Leading ethically means everyone is aware of the mission, vision, values, and goals that set a standard for how people will conduct themselves to accomplish the company's objectives. In these ethical companies, decisions are made by everyone, both followers and leaders, based on the standards created collectively and set forth to guide them. Leaders in these organizations make decisions based on what is best for the common good, not just for themselves.

An ethical leader doesn't say one thing and then behave differently. Their actions are aligned with their stated values. There is no hiding from their actions. The leader is transparent so that everyone can witness when they aren't being consistent or doing what they said they would.

This type of leadership is increasingly important as Gen Z is more likely to hold their leaders accountable for ethical behavior. Anticipated to make up 25 percent of the workforce by 2025, Gen Z employees start with feelings of distrust for leaders and only make a shift to trust when it is earned with transparency and authenticity. This generation has strong values and ethics and is inflexible in their beliefs. They cannot be intimidated into changing their views. Gen Z followers are also accustomed to being exposed to a variety of thoughts and interactions with diverse people throughout their lifetimes, and they demand adaptability from their leadership. For example, if there is a negative news story about a client with whom the company is doing business, the Gen Z followers will insist the leader take this information into account when deciding to continue to work with the client.[40]

The disconnect

When what a leader says and does are disconnected, followers notice the lack of integrity. Even when following through on what they say is hard or unpleasant, the leader must do so because doing what they say matters. Inconsistencies between words and actions lead to a loss of power. Lapses in integrity, even if small, damage a leader's reputation, relationships, and trust from followers. There is no reason for followers to believe a leader when they aren't known for doing what they say. And when leaders lose this power, they can no longer influence others to follow them, no matter how hard they try to rationalize their actions. Conversely, when the leader is direct and operates with no deception, exaggeration, or waffling, the trust that emerges gives them power. This power creates influence, which is one of the greatest tools a leader has in their toolbox.

Trust is eroded en masse

Today, in this highly connected world, where leaders' words can be broadcast far beyond the intended audience, it has become even more important for leaders to keep their word. Look no further than political leaders who make many promises while campaigning before the realities of being in office and being unable to affect the change they promised set in. In George H. W. Bush's acceptance speech for the 1988 presidential nomination, he made a big promise. In contrast to his opponent who said he would raise taxes, Bush said he wouldn't allow that to happen. He said he knew he would be pushed by lawmakers, but he would push back. His promise culminated in a line that became famous: "…I'll say to them, 'Read my lips: no new taxes.'"

Later, after taking office and facing the realities of a stalled US economy, President Bush finally conceded that one of the measures needed to address the economic woes of the country was to increase tax revenues. The next day's headline in the *New York Post* read: "Read My Lips…I Lied!" Even when promises are made in the heat of the moment, leaders must acknowledge the commitment they are making and be cognizant of the ramifications of welching on that commitment. Trust is built bit by bit but eroded en masse.

When German Chancellor Angela Merkel observed the Fukushima, Japan nuclear disaster in 2011, she pledged to phase out nuclear power in Germany.[41] Though previously a supporter of her country's use of nuclear power, she was moved by the unintended impact on the Fukushima nuclear plant from the 9.0 magnitude earthquake and subsequent tsunami that led to a meltdown of the nuclear reactor and the release of radioactive materials. She was able to convince the German government to pass a law to eliminate nuclear power within a decade. The decision wasn't universally popular, and it wasn't easy to make the changes, but the goal was accomplished. In April 2023, the last three remaining nuclear power plants in Germany were closed, completing the transition away from nuclear power.[42] Merkel's leadership and commitment to the cause made this possible and was one factor that contributed to her long tenure as Germany's chancellor.

A leader who upholds their promises has loyal and dedicated followers. Bonds are formed with employees when a leader shows they are true to their word. When a leader is perceived as being honorable, honorable people are attracted to them. Followers see their leaders as a reflection of their own character and reliability. For a leader to successfully inspire followers, keeping their word and doing what they say they will is essential. When a leader doesn't treat their word as their bond, they give up the opportunity for trust and influence.

Leaders sometimes say things they don't mean or can't deliver on. Has this happened to you? What would you have done differently? What did you learn? Who is a leader you admire who keeps their word?

Sometimes keeping your word requires a large dose of courage. In order to build your ability to lead, you must show courage—in a variety of ways—which leads us to our next characteristic.

Chapter 12
Courage

Not all humans are wired to take risks. Leaders must often face their fears and act in spite of them. While anyone can appear brave when situations are easy and the stakes are low, too often, fear pushes us into inaction. We rationalize why our fears are well-founded. We justify our stalling. We avoid the problem at hand. But a leader who is intimidated by challenges loses their authority to lead. Courage is one of the most important virtues—and a key characteristic—of being a leader others want to follow.

The following questions may come up: Can we lead when the situation is threatening and the outcome is uncertain? Can we stand by our beliefs and convictions even when others disagree? Can we be sure we are behaving in a way that benefits the greater good and doesn't merely protect or stroke our egos?

Courage in leadership

Through a lens of courage, a leader sees opportunities for self-improvement and growth in challenging situations. They behave in ways that are true to their values and vision, even if it is hard to stick to their convictions. With this strength, the leader with courage is able to weather adversity and show their strength to their followers. They have the discipline to be decisive and not waffle. This doesn't mean they will never change direction if the situation calls for it, but it does mean they will stick with their decision until the results indicate it's time to change.

The leader with courage sifts through the stimuli and commits to action. They have the ability to say "Here is our goal. This is why we're taking this action." When it's clear this path won't get us to our intended goals, we can shift direction. Until then, we are committed, even if it becomes challenging.

A leader with courage acts decisively and takes action despite the anticipation of consequences. They make difficult decisions after gathering input and data. They give their followers the opportunity to share their opinions and advice, but recognize the decision is ultimately up to them as the leader. This doesn't mean the leader always knows the action they are taking is the right one, but they are willing to take the chance and stand by their decision, because they know that a lack of decision-making will lead to a loss in authority.

When an expedition leader takes their group to summit Mount Everest, they know it is their job to get climbers safely to the summit. Each expedition requires hundreds of little and big decisions informed by weather, the condition of the climbers, equipment, and more. Each of these decisions—those made and those not made—determine the likelihood of accomplishing their summit goal. Leaders worth following know it's all their decisions, big and small, that determine their team's likelihood of achieving their vision.

How to communicate with courage

Sometimes the leader needs courage not to make the decision but to communicate their decision to followers. By clearly articulating the reasons for a particular decision, leaders increase the chances followers will join them. Sharing the reasons for a decision doesn't mean the leader is defending the decision, but instead, they are tying it to the larger purpose of the team. This becomes particularly important when the decision is unpopular.

At the start of my tenure as the CEO of Women's Bean Project, we had two businesses. One was the original food manufacturing business that exists to this day, and the other was a catering business. The organization had gotten into catering almost accidentally when a family member of the founder asked them to provide prepared soup for their wedding. From this simple beginning, the business grew to provide prepared soup and boxed lunches to nonprofits and churches in the community.

By the time I became the CEO, the catering business had several catering events each week but only employed one or two program participants and didn't keep them busy full-time. Overall, the Bean Project was losing money, but because the accounting for the two business units was clumped together, it was hard to see where the losses stemmed from. With a new director of finance, we created a cost center accounting system, which quickly revealed that not only did the catering business lose money, the more catering we did, the more money we'd lose. The business wasn't busy enough to get materials in bulk, so we were paying retail prices for many of our ingredients. Added to this challenge was an inconsistency in quality. To save money, our catering manager sometimes ordered cheap white bread, which after being wrapped in cling wrap, arrived to the customer smooshed nearly beyond recognition. And because the client base was churches and nonprofits, we were limited by the belief we couldn't raise our prices to make a profit.

There was also a lot of love for the catering business from customers, donors, and the board of directors. Everyone wanted us to continue catering their events with our bargain basement prices. I decided we would work to turn around the business to become a profit center for the organization and create jobs for more than just one or two women. For eighteen months we made adjustments to increase sales and try to stem the losses to no avail. Our product quality wasn't good enough to justify higher prices, and we couldn't seem to create consistent improvement in the quality of our boxed lunches.

One morning, after looking at a financial statement showing yet another month of losses, I realized that all the energy going into this business we were clearly not very good at was impeding our ability to grow the business we were good at: the bean soup and baking mixes that we were selling in hundreds of stores across the country. It occurred to me that if we could make the same amount of revenue in our food manufacturing business as we were making in our catering business, it would not only be profitable, but it would also employ about a dozen additional women each year. Since the purpose of our business was to employ women experiencing chronic unemployment so they could move to mainstream employment in the community, suddenly the decision was no longer a business decision but a mission decision.

I gathered our leadership team to share my belief we should shutter the catering business and bulleted out my rationale. Within the span of fifteen minutes, we created a plan to complete the jobs on the calendar, communicate the change, and refer future business to other catering companies. Once the plan was created, I made the comment to the team that it had only taken us fifteen minutes to shutter the entire business, and one of my teammates laughed and said, "Eighteen months and fifteen minutes." He was right. It was a decision that was a long time coming, but once made, was not as challenging to implement as I might have thought. And with the mission clarity, it felt easy to justify and communicate widely.

Even so, implementing the decision required more courage than I anticipated. Though the board of directors accepted the decision, many customers questioned us. For years they continued to reach out and request our catering services. We developed bullet-pointed messaging our team could share when we received calls because some customers questioned our decision and demanded an explanation as to why we had shuttered the business. There were weeks when it was tempting to relaunch catering because it felt as though all the customers who hadn't called us while it was still operating were now trying to hire us. Fortunately, we had a collective agreement to stick with our decision and the courage of our convictions that it was the right thing for the company. Within a year, we more than made up the revenue lost from catering in our food manufacturing business.

Volodymyr Zelenskyy's courageous leadership

A recent example of courageous leadership was displayed by Ukrainian President Volodymyr Zelenskyy. In 2022, like many people around the world, I watched with disbelief as Russia invaded Ukraine. And, like others, I have been in awe of Zelenskyy's response to the invasion as he has led his fellow Ukrainians through a war. President Zelenskyy has epitomized the qualities of a courageous leader. He is honest and frank in spite of the pressure he is under. Though offered the opportunity to flee his country, he declined, with the retort that he needed ammunition, not a ride.

Today we seldom see public leaders who show the kind of courage Zelenskyy has displayed. He has exhibited the ability to rise to the challenge and act in the face of an overwhelming foreign foe. He has demonstrated how to face conflict head-on. I suspect the Ukrainian people are better able to fight because their president is showing such incredible courage.

President Zelenskyy displays the courage of his convictions that, despite incredible hardship inflicted on his fellow compatriots as they oppose Russia, his actions are warranted. He has effectively communicated that the fight for Ukraine matters because it represents a fight for democracy. His displays of courage are an example for his people and for the rest of the world. I have viewed a number of videos of his speeches, some translated into English, some not. For those without translation, I have been left to watch his nonverbal cues. He is somber, of course, but he is also direct and clear, resolute and firm. He speaks slowly, deliberately, and emphatically, coming across as genuine and trustworthy. He presents the facts while appearing brave, defiant, and proud. After bombings of the capital city Kyiv, he posted a video of himself alongside other Ukrainian officials saying, "We're still here!"[43]

When a reporter asked Zelenskyy if he realized he was becoming iconic, Zelenskyy responded, "I'm not iconic. Ukraine is iconic."[44] There is genuine humility in how he speaks that people respond to. His strength is inspirational. One translator on live German TV found the courage Zelenskyy displayed to be so moving he broke down in tears and was unable to finish his interpretation.[45] For many reasons, Zelenskyy is a leader who has moved far beyond politics and has touched the hearts and minds of people around the world. One of these reasons is his courage in continuing to lead his country despite unimaginable hardship.

One might assume Zelenskyy was elected because he had previously displayed courage, but in fact, Zelenskyy's background as a comedian and reality TV star in Ukraine did not indicate he would emerge as a courageous leader. When he won the presidential election, the expectations of him were low, and there was little to suggest he would rise to the occasion during a crisis.

And yet, it is hard to think of many well-known leaders today who have been as effective at rallying their country and support for their people.

Of course, few people will have the opportunity to display courage in the way Zelenskyy has done. Most decisions we make as leaders are not as existential. Yet, too often, leaders make decisions out of fear, rather than in spite of it—fear of being wrong, of losing credibility, of losing our jobs.

As leaders, what we do with the everyday situations we are faced with is what defines us. What might occur if our default was to act from a place of courage? An essential first step might be to fight our natural inclination to make the safe choice. If we act despite feeling afraid and speak up according to our beliefs, would we then have the conviction to stick with our decisions? Would we be humble enough to recognize our role in the decision?

The amazing thing about choosing courage over fear is that the more one does it, the easier it becomes and the more one becomes a leader worth following. Even small acts of courage inspire others. Acting courageously is like building muscles. Just as in strength training, it is not in the onetime workout a person becomes stronger but in the cumulative moments of weightlifting, repeated over and over again, that one builds strength.

Courage can be a defining quality in a leader. Certainly, the absence of courage can be a leader's undoing. It is displayed not only in grand gestures, but also in little moments when a leader makes a decision and stands by what they believe.

Let's explore the first lesson of courage: to act in the face of fear.

Chapter 13

Act in the Face of Fear

Nelson Mandela, a leader in the anti-apartheid movement and the first Black president of South Africa, said courage is not the absence of fear but the triumph over it.[46] A key aspect of courageous leadership is mastering one's fear—being afraid but acting anyway. Mandela knew this. Throughout his opposition of apartheid, he faced fear and discomfort, yet took action in the face of that fear, accepting the consequences, including twenty-seven years in prison, because he believed the purpose of ending apartheid to be greater than himself.

I don't know how Mandela analyzed the situations he was in and determined to act anyway, but I have a strategy I have developed for my own life. I call it my Park Bench Analysis. When faced with a decision that scares me, I imagine myself at eighty years old, sitting on a park bench and looking back on my life. From that bench, reflecting on my past decisions, I ask myself, will I regret not taking this chance? If fear is the only reason I might not take the leap, I know that's not good enough. It's okay to be afraid or uncomfortable, but I need to act anyway. Courage is not about being fearless but feeling the fear and acting in spite of it.

Expectations have changed

Just as cultural norms have changed over time, what followers need from leaders has shifted as well. Today's drivers of change include technological advancement, the increasing interconnectivity of the world, and the impact of constant media access. And the pace of change has accelerated, making it impossible for leaders to have enough information to feel certain all the time, yet they are still expected to act. I recall how overwhelmed I felt at the beginning of the COVID pandemic when information felt both abundant and scarce. We didn't know much about the virus at the time, but there was a daily bombardment of details and new requirements for businesses being broadcast. I recall trying to consume as much information as I could as quickly as possible because my team was looking to me for information and directives about how we would continue to operate.

I noted what my team members wanted ran counter to my go-to management style. Typically, I sit with the team, and we discuss our goals and agree on our desired outcomes. If, after review, the planned activities don't seem like they will accomplish our stated objectives, we discuss alternative plans that more closely align with our desired outcomes, but the decisions about how to move closer to the stated goals is my team's, not mine. It isn't a hands-off approach, but it is intended to keep me out of unnecessary details and allow others to feel ownership.

Throughout the pandemic, this wasn't what my team was seeking. They wanted to be told what to do: when to show up for work, when to stay at home, when to wear masks, and when to get tested. They wanted decisions and reassurance.

I remember feeling emotionally and mentally crushed by the pressure because I felt just as overwhelmed as they did, but it seemed as though there wasn't space for me to feel that way or let others know I felt that way. Too many people were looking to me to know the answers and convey certainty I didn't feel. I also felt that everyone had become much less tolerant of my imperfections and lack of knowledge, unwilling to give grace in a time of such crisis. Though I might have preferred to withdraw and focus exclusively on my family, I realized I had to sit with the discomfort and fear, gather as much information as possible, make decisions, and lead.

Sitting with discomfort and making a decision anyway is often challenging for leaders. I didn't make decisions during the pandemic because I knew more than others, but because others were looking to me to take in the information and give guidance for how we would respond. The team expected me to tell them if we could stay open and keep working. As a food manufacturer, we were considered an essential business, so the answer was yes. Then they wanted me to share a plan for keeping everyone safe and develop guidelines for how our business would operate within the recommended restrictions from the mayor of Denver, the governor of Colorado, the health department, the Centers for Disease Control, and more.

Shortly after the lockdowns and restrictions began, people began losing jobs at record rates, and there was much speculation about the impact on the economy. I watched a webinar from a well-respected fundraising consultant on how nonprofit organizations could weather the anticipated economic downturn. She started with a statement I found compelling. She said, "Don't kid yourself. Any problems you have today existed before. COVID has just brought them to the forefront." I was emboldened by this statement. Why was I afraid? The problems I was confronting were just issues that had been sitting on the sidelines waiting for an opportunity to arise. COVID merely opened the door for them. I found her message liberating, and while the challenges didn't go away, my attitude toward them and my belief in my ability to handle them improved.

The psychology of fear

Everyone feels fear. Fear is a primitive emotional response designed to keep us out of danger. While fear is intended to assist with self-preservation, the way it manifests can vary greatly, depending on past experience. When interacting with others, it can be helpful to realize that most people are constantly dealing with fear on some level. It could be the fear of being wrong or looking bad in front of others. Or the fear of making a bad decision, being abandoned, or becoming financially dependent on others.

Regardless of how fears manifest, at their root they are about past experience or self-preservation. When leaders notice they are feeling stuck or unable to make a decision, getting to the root of the fear can help. Knowing oneself well enough to identify when fear is getting in the way is essential. Understanding the source of the fear and naming it is a good first step. The next step requires looking at how fear is leading to a delayed decision. Recognizing how much of the fear is real and how much is unfounded can help a leader move away from their inaction. Overcoming fear to make a decision or take action is essential because not acting in the face of fear begets more fear-based behavior. A leader loses their credibility when they become known as someone who lets fear drive them.

Be afraid and act anyway

A leader must be able to overcome their fears and act anyway. What they do in the face of fear will define them. Showing courage is not extraordinary, and it doesn't imply a lack of fear. Daily acts of courage in the face of fear positively affect the team. Seeing a courageous leader in action creates opportunities for a culture of courage within the team and builds loyalty from followers. When team members face their fears together, they feel more loyal to one another, and their performance is better.

Being afraid and acting in spite of it requires a boldness that followers are seeking. This is the kind of leadership that inspires others to follow. Leaders worth following don't lack fear; they merely act in the face of it.

When have you been afraid but acted anyway? What was the result? Are there times you wish you'd taken action in the face of fear?

Just as we are wired to avoid things we are fearful of, we also instinctively prefer to avoid conflict. But a leader worth following doesn't run away from conflict. The next lesson addresses this tendency.

Chapter 14

Don't Run Away from Conflict

Just as humans are wired to avoid things they are fearful of, we also instinctively prefer to avoid the discomfort that comes from conflict. But a leader worth following knows conflict can't be avoided. They know how to lead despite conflict by navigating difficult conversations in a way that allows everyone to walk away feeling respected. Followers want their leaders to be willing to face conflict situations and expect them to understand and navigate both healthy and unhealthy conflict within their teams.

Conflict in the workplace can be either productive or unproductive, and the leader must be able to lead through both. Leaders worth following know conflict is inevitable, and the key is how it's addressed. Productive conflict encourages healthy discussion. Team members must be led to stretch their communication capabilities and learn how to express their needs and concerns in productive ways. This helps make the team stronger and creates an environment in which different perspectives and ideas can be shared. While there might still be tension, it can be healthy in a way that allows for better results because it creates space for a variety of ideas to be presented and considered.

Conversely, in unproductive conflict, people forget the bigger picture and the overarching goals of the group or organization and begin to focus on their own egos and being right. Rather than entertaining multiple ideas, they tend to focus on one idea over others, often based on their preference for the person presenting rather than the idea itself. This results in making the situation about one person winning over another. It pits one idea against another: not only is *my* idea good, but *your* idea is bad. The long-term effect of this type of conflict is to diminish psychological safety and trust while morale suffers.

When conflict is not addressed productively, things that seem little are ignored and small aggressions between team members are tolerated. When conflict builds without being addressed, situations become personal and behavior among team members turns to blaming.

How to help the team

Too many leaders use avoidance as their go-to response when conflict is brewing. Or the leader focuses on unrelated problems because they don't have the courage to confront the individual causing the conflict. But when an issue isn't addressed, it merely festers. Everyone can see when an employee displays unproductive and disrespectful behavior. The entire team suffers when unresolved conflict is present because eventually it will extend beyond the team members having the conflict and lead to a loss in the leader's credibility. When a leader ignores or is reluctant to address conflict, followers become resentful, or they give up on the team and begin to operate on their own.

Sometimes when there is conflict among team members, it isn't appropriate—or in large companies, even possible—for the leader to be directly involved in the resolution; instead, the leader's role is to serve as coach and guide. This is particularly true when the conflict occurs between two people when the leader is not present. In these situations, the leader must start by acknowledging there is a problem, even if they didn't witness it. Asking questions of each person involved is a good way to start, such as saying, "I sense tension between the two of you. Can you share with me what is happening? I'm curious about what is going on." Further, asking if they have talked to one another about their concerns, asking what happened when they did so, and what feedback they received in return can help each individual begin to see a path to resolving the conflict on their own.

In these situations, the leader must resist the urge to try and solve the problem for the followers. Instead, the leader should be evaluating the underlying source of the conflict. Is it caused because of an interpersonal problem? Is there an issue with a system or process in the organization that is unintentionally pitting the two team members against each other? Is the conflict affecting the business's ability to be successful? Have the two individuals attempted unsuccessfully to reach a resolution? Is it time for the leader to get involved?

One Monday morning, I had just finished a meeting and was walking past one of our conference rooms when I noticed eight staff members crammed into a room that typically hosted four or five people. The looks on everyone's faces were grim. At the time, our staff only consisted of fourteen people, so I thought it was unusual to have so many people in the room at one time. There were several teams represented, including the program services team, the food production team, and human resources. However, there wasn't just one person from each team—the entire departments were in the room. I made a mental note and moved on with my day.

The next day, during a one-on-one meeting with a direct report—one of the people who had been in the room the prior day—she shared that she was ready to quit because of what had occurred in that crammed-room meeting. She felt disrespected by her coworkers and didn't want to stay in a place that would allow such behavior. I was alarmed by such a dramatic statement and began asking questions.

I learned the meeting had been called to make a decision about firing one of our program participants. Because of the nature of the Bean Project's work, it was not unusual for cross-functional teams to be involved in discussions about program participants. Women who participated in the program were also employed as production assistants. In that capacity, they were supervised by the food production team. When the food production team experienced difficulty with an individual, they worked with human resources for performance improvement coaching. Additionally, the food production team could enlist the program services team to help address issues that arose because of challenges occurring outside of work. I often thought of it as the production team's job to identify the problematic behavior, or the what, such as tardiness, while the program services team addressed the why behind the behavior. For example, why is the employee arriving late to work each day, and how might the team help her address that issue so she can be on time?

In theory, this division of labor sounded good, but the reality was that it often pitted the staff members against one another. The production team didn't want a problem employee on the production floor because of the impact on productivity, so they tended to swiftly refer women to human resources rather than coach the women themselves. In the course of staff members' work with each woman, information was sometimes shared with the program team that felt inappropriate for the production team or HR to know. Without meaning to, we had created a dynamic between teams that was ripe for conflict.

As I gathered further information, it became apparent that team members arrived at the Meeting of Eight, as we began to call it, with different—and conflicting—agendas. Some attendees had already decided what should happen, conducted side conversations before the meeting, and planned to walk into the room merely to inform the others of their decision instead of getting input. Apparently, the meeting quickly devolved into personal attacks with some raising their voices, others not feeling heard, and some who just sat and observed.

While I realized I had only heard about a small portion of the dysfunction happening between these teams, I was dismayed to learn what had transpired. I could see that across departments, team members' goals weren't aligned, the meeting had become personal, and the big picture—the purpose behind our work— had been lost. For those in the room that day, it became about being right, not doing what was right for the program participants. As the leader, I knew it was my job to ensure the conflict and the systemic issues that had led to the conflict were addressed. It was very tempting to get involved, but I also had to recognize I wasn't equipped with the skills to handle such complicated conflict on my own. It was time for some external expertise. After making a few inquiries, I was able to find an expert in nonviolent communication to help the team heal through restorative conversations and learn skills to work better together in the future.

My response to this situation was to choose to be the coach, not the mediator. I recognized the problems within the team had escalated to the point of needing mediation, and I knew that wasn't a role I could fulfill. That didn't mean I was hands off. In the introductory meeting with the expert, I shared my expectations with the team for how they would participate in the restorative work for the betterment of their relationships and the organization. I told the Meeting of Eight participants that I knew I didn't have the skills to solve the issues that had emerged and that the best solutions would be ones they developed together. After introducing the expert to the group, I bowed out and allowed the process to evolve. Handing the responsibility for resolving the issue to the team was not a way to avoid the conflict, but instead required courage to acknowledge I was out of my depth in such a complicated situation.

The leader's role as empathetic coach

There are situations, such as the Meeting of Eight issue, in which serving as coach is the best and most courageous role for the leader whose team is having conflict. This includes coaching the individuals involved to have the courage to address the conflict directly, rather than letting it fester, or allowing people to vent their frustrations, then redirecting the conversation to brainstorm possible productive resolutions. Coaching means that the leader sits on the sidelines, checking on progress and providing additional empathetic coaching as needed.

Empathy is the capacity of the heart to understand another's point of view. When a leader displays empathy, they start with an understanding of the experience and perspective of another person. I know when I am able to tap into empathy, I can begin to understand the emotional patterns of my teammates, what gets in the way of their success, and what helps them succeed. I can help them work through defeatist thoughts and develop new patterns of thinking.

Once, when my sales director said—for what seemed like the hundredth time—that she wasn't detail oriented, I interrupted her and said I disagreed, then proceeded to give her examples of when she had been focused on details. I added that we all forget things at times, but when she claimed she wasn't detail oriented, it might really be a way to give herself room to fail rather than succeed. She risked damaging her credibility with others who can't relate. It was just the shot in the arm she needed. From then on, she focused on the ways she was able to address details, rather than those she occasionally struggled with.

Modeling empathy requires physical, mental, and emotional involvement from the leader. The empathetic leader coach leans in and pays attention to the person, staying entirely engaged in the conversation with eye contact. They actively listen, with responses like "I think I hear you saying X. Is that accurate?" They watch for nonverbal cues to intuit if their words and body language match, and seek ways to address the disconnect when they don't. The leader's focus is on learning more about the person and their perspective.

The empathetic coach asks about the follower's needs and if they have considered the needs of the other person involved in the conflict. When necessary, the leader sets guidelines for how the team will engage, insisting followers respond to the conflict in a way that is specific to the situation, not based on preconceived ideas of what is right. I often say there are three sides to every story: your side, my side, and the truth. Making an effort to understand each person's motives, concerns, and perspective helps the leader be an empathetic coach.

When the leader needs to be there

Sometimes the leader needs to be directly involved in addressing conflict. Too often, leaders wait for the perfect set of circumstances to have hard conversations instead of having the courage to address issues swiftly. We are all imperfect humans and bring our imperfections to every interaction, so if we wait for everything to be perfect, we won't address the issue when it's necessary (or at all). The leader worth following exhibits several behaviors in effective conflict management. They are candid, directly addressing the issue that needs to be discussed. They make it clear that productive conflict is okay and being respectful is a requirement. They also depersonalize conflict by recognizing that even if they are involved, it isn't only about them. The rest of the team is also affected as conflict between any two people affects more than just those involved.

Learning more about conflict styles can be helpful in improving the inclination toward addressing conflict. The Thomas-Kilmann Conflict Mode Instrument is a tool that asks the respondent how they usually behave when there is conflict.[47] The results help individuals recognize which style is their go-to when they approach conflict, as well as the pros and cons of their style. One style is not better than another and the results show that different styles are useful in various situations. By knowing there are alternative responses to conflict, the individual can consider if there is a better style to be used to address a particular situation.

The styles are presented along two axes of assertiveness and cooperativeness which serve to identify five conflict styles, including competing (assertive, uncooperative), avoiding (unassertive, uncooperative), accommodating (unassertive, cooperative), collaborating (assertive, cooperative), and compromising (moderately assertive, moderately cooperative). Understanding team members' styles in this context can help with working through conflict productively. For instance, when a team member is competing, it is important to get to the root of why they feel unheard or minimized, as if they think their opinion isn't being considered or valued. Or, if they are avoiding, help them understand how that style is affecting the rest of the team.

The paradox of conflict

Though the leader wants to inspire people to follow them, they cannot lose sight of the fact that their responsibility is to the organization, not to the individual. The leader must sometimes choose the solution that is best for the company over what might be better for the individual. They have to have the courage to decide when it is necessary to part with a team member when it seems that the conflict cannot be resolved in a way that works for the organization. Despite the challenge of making this decision, it can be done in a respectful way. Sometimes, when a conflict can't be resolved and it's time to part ways with a team member, I use the saying "bless and release." It's a way to think about separating from a teammate with whom a resolution can't be found. Acknowledging that lack of resolution is not healthy for the company, the leader can also indicate there is no ill will, but that the decision for separation is being made for the organization's benefit.

My executive coach once suggested that when I'm preparing for a tough conversation, I ask myself, "Am I committed to this person's success? Can I be committed to this person's success and the organization's success simultaneously?" Asking these questions in advance requires me to consider how I need to show up to the conversation, as well as how I want to conduct myself throughout. If I am committed to the person, I feel I will work more earnestly to resolve the conflict. Conversely, if I were to show up without this commitment, I may be more inclined to bless and release them.

Living with the reality that conflict can exist in healthy relationships, knowing how to identify positive and negative conflict, and then either coaching toward resolution or resolving directly is a talent found in leaders worth following. Ignoring conflict doesn't work. Effective leaders don't allow conflict to go unchecked or unresolved. Facing conflict and following through to resolution requires courage.

What is your go-to conflict management style? How do you support your team in resolving conflict? How do you show up when you are committed to another's success?

While some leaders avoid conflict, others avoid decisions. Neither is effective. The next chapter addresses decision-making. To be a leader worth following, you need to have courage to make decisions—and stick with them.

Chapter 15
Have the Courage of Your Convictions

Some leaders are afraid to make decisions. They waffle, pander, or hide behind the need to continually gather more information. I have a very smart friend who has led several organizations. She is analytical by nature and good at asking questions to gather the information she believes she needs. However, she struggles to commit. Often, she has decided what action she would like to take yet continues to gather information instead of implementing. She has shared with me that her team accuses her of having decided but being afraid to take action.

After years of coaching her informally, I believe she hesitates to own the fact that, as the leader, the decisions are hers to make—and the consequences are hers to live with. I adore this friend, and when she shares with me the feedback she's gotten from her team about her inability to commit to a decision, I struggle not to pile on and tell her I agree with them. Instead, I try to coach her by asking what might be getting in her way, or, if she was forced to decide right then, what would she do? I often leave our conversations doubting she'll commit to the decision at hand.

One of the scariest things for a leader can be the pressure to make the "right" decision. The feeling of being responsible for the important decisions can be overwhelming and some leaders believe all their decisions must be made alone. Add to that the fact that many decisions don't have a single right answer. The key to making a decision is to make the best possible one with the information available, but even then, which one is the best possible?

Fortunately, there is a strategy that can be deployed for making decisions a leader can feel they are able to stick with. The first step is to understand what decision needs to be made because if the leader isn't clear, they will struggle to be effective. Next is to determine what data and other facts are needed in order to make the decision. For instance, does the leader need to have more information about the current situation? Are there gaps that exist, and how might the needed data be gathered? Once the available data is gathered, the leader must consider options, weighing one versus another to see which solution might be better. Part of this exploration may include getting others' opinions, bearing their own biases in mind. Does the input they're requesting come from a self-serving place? When it comes time to make the decision, the leader who inspires others will also recognize where their own biases and emotions are impacting them.

Once the decision is made, it's time to stick with it and learn from the outcome. Committing to a decision means the leader openly communicates what they have decided. They must exude confidence in their decision and know the decision was made based on the best information available. The leader must avoid saying things like "I decided, but I might change my mind if others don't like the decision." They must have the courage to stand by their decision.

The impact of decisiveness

Before I became the CEO of Women's Bean Project in 2003, the board had stepped in to help the organization recover from a financial crisis. Though I was aware there were challenges, from the outside it was hard to know how severe they were. Once I started work as the CEO, the board stepped back, partially from relief that someone else was in charge, and partly because they had been doing the heavy lifting of making the decisions required to keep the doors open and they were fatigued. As I assessed the situation from the inside, I felt the urgency to make changes and set us on a path to sustainability. Each day I found problems, and though it's likely none of them individually were enough to have created the crisis, when combined, they were potentially lethal to the organization.

It was hard not to be overwhelmed by the gravity of the obstacles in front of me. By taking the job, I took responsibility for making payroll every two weeks. I raised my hand to lead WBP's salvation while not really understanding what that meant. I began making decisions to address the most pressing issues, such as cash flow. Before long, I started hearing from people in the community who disagreed with my decisions.

The Bean Project is a bit of a community darling. Part of the organization's long-term success has been because it captured the imagination and support of so many people with its social enterprise model. It is a business, and the better the business does, the more women can be served. And when women successfully complete the program, they change the trajectory of their lives. A result of being a program participant at the Bean Project can lead to a long-term impact on the community through their children and extended family.

The community knew this and was invested in our success. However, they were also unaware of the details behind the challenges we faced. Like a firefighter who must address the little blazes to keep the full-blown fire from taking over again, I had to take many small actions. Frequently, I made a decision based on the limited information I could gather and what felt like the best course of action at that moment. I can't say I always knew how things would turn out. Often, all I had was the courage of my convictions that I was choosing the best option at that time. More often than not, I was correct, and slowly, we changed our course toward a more stable organization. But even when I was mistaken about a decision, I was able to take the new information into account to shift and adapt.

Still, having people from outside the day-to-day operations feel empowered to have input on my decisions was unsettling. Having never had a job where anyone outside of my organization felt they could weigh in on my actions, I found the judgment from others—people who I was depending on for financial support in the form of grants and donations—disconcerting and disheartening. I overcame the temptation to justify individual decisions and instead communicated my conviction that we were doing what was necessary to change the trajectory of the Bean Project. As we achieved more and more success, the critical voices quieted and the whispers of congratulations became louder and louder.

In retrospect, I don't remember which decisions ended up being wrong or for which I was criticized, but I vividly recall needing to find the courage required to stand by my decisions and stare down the criticism. One reason I could do this was because I knew that if a decision I'd made didn't work out, we had the wherewithal to shift and make a different choice. It's one thing to commit to a decision and another to hold to it stubbornly when it proves to be ineffective. Courage is required to stay the course and adapt as needed.

The courage of your convictions

Having the courage of your convictions means you are doing what needs to be done even if it is unpopular or questioned by others. Even before the criticism begins, some leaders, like my friend, struggle to be decisive. They give in to uncertainty or make a decision from a place of fear and, when questioned, have a hard time sticking with their decision.

Or, they gather the information and data but fail to take a stand and end up in analysis paralysis. The leader in this situation might try to tell themself that no decision is better than a wrong decision, but this isn't true. No decision *is* a decision. One way to overcome analysis paralysis includes giving oneself a deadline to decide; for instance, deciding to sleep on it and decide in the morning before going into work. Other times, when I think I know my decision but feel something is holding me back from committing, I go for a run, call a friend, or read—anything to disengage my mind from the situation for a bit. When I do this, I invariably gain clarity and can commit to my choice.

Some leaders get overwhelmed by what seems to be an unlimited number of options. This dilemma comes from not fully analyzing the choices. If good data is gathered and the leader seeks input while also considering what decision will move the company closer to its vision, it becomes clear the choices are not unlimited.

What does courage mean?

A leader worth following has backbone and genuine convictions and is comfortable with who they are. They don't get stuck worrying about what others will think; they are able to make tough decisions without waffling. Sticking with a decision requires confidence without being overconfident. Leaders understand that arrogance damages their followers' confidence and ultimately leads them to withhold their trust and loyalty.

None of this is to say that decision-making is easy. The leader must be flexible enough to think about a variety of solutions and humble enough to admit when they are wrong. They must be open-minded and able to sit in the ambiguity that exists between being willing to change their mind and having the wisdom to stand by their convictions.

The Amazon dream

Jeff Bezos dreamed of creating an "everything store" that would serve as an intermediary between customers and manufacturers. To do this, he knew he had to start with a product niche. After analyzing several options, he chose to build his online platform around selling books for three reasons: one copy of a book is the same as any other, the book distribution world was very consolidated, and an online store could differentiate itself by offering many more books than a physical bookstore.[48]

Amazon launched as "Earth's Biggest Bookstore" and expanded from there. Starting with books was a great first decision, and many additional decisions, including a focus on continuously improving the customer experience, led to Amazon's eventual success. I recall how Bezos was criticized for how much time and money was required to make Amazon profitable, he maintained the courage of his convictions that he was headed in the right direction.

The writer of a 1999 article published in *Barron's*, a magazine that covers US financial information, said the idea that Amazon would change the world was silly. The critic said the only successful internet companies would be firms selling their own products directly, not "middlemen" like Amazon. Bezos tweeted a clip of this article in 2021 as a lesson in dealing with criticism. Had he listened to the opinion of this writer (and likely others at the time), he would have never proceeded with building Amazon to what it is today.[49]

Jeff Bezos never doubted Amazon's potential. As the dot-com bubble burst in the early 2000s and Amazon continued to lose money, Bezos continued believing—because he was focused on the data—that they needed to scale to be successful. And he made his leadership decisions accordingly. The criticism from the media and the business community could have led Bezos to make different decisions or backtrack on decisions previously made. However, he had the courage to continuously believe he had the right strategy for the long run and that conviction led to the Amazon we know today.[50]

Decide and be flexible

While a leader must have a firm foundation for decision-making and sticking with those decisions, they must also ensure they have the courage to be agile enough to change course if necessary. A good decision is never about doing what will be popular but about doing the right thing—regardless of if it is difficult or hard to stand by. When a leader sticks with what they believe to be the best decision for the organization, they build trust and respect. A leader who is willing to sacrifice popularity in the short run for the right thing in the long run is showing the courage of their convictions.

When do you struggle to make decisions? Do you have a hard time sticking with those decisions? How do you know you're making the right choice?

The final lesson in courage is how to remain confident while displaying humility and vulnerability.

Chapter 16
Finding Strength In Humility

Hubris makes a leader overconfident in the face of risk. The more arrogantly a leader behaves, particularly if it feels outsized to the situation, the greater the risk of followers losing confidence in them. Followers value humility and vulnerability, and leaders have more power when they are tethered to these qualities.

Too often, leaders feel they must have the answers and leave little room for input from their followers. But this style of leadership is outdated and ends up making the leader seem arrogant and overbearing. Followers who are inspired by their leaders know that the leader values them enough to ask for their opinion. An essential way a leader can demonstrate how they value their followers is by overcoming the compulsion to behave as if they know everything and don't need input. Solutions developed collectively between leaders and followers are stronger and more apt to get buy-in.

Asking questions and requesting input shows vulnerability and demonstrates the leader is open to help, serving to send a strong signal that the leader is trusting. By giving trust, the leader is more likely to get trust in return. Rather than relying solely on their own knowledge or experience, a leader who asks good questions helps their team connect with them and builds a culture of collaboration.

The art of asking questions

There is art to asking good questions, and the more one does it, the better one becomes. Leaders who are focused on asking questions rather than providing answers must commit to listening before they speak. When trying to innovate or resolve an issue, "why" questions help the team understand the problem, and "how" questions spark brainstorming. "How might we" questions get at the implementation and are typically asked last because they help the team determine which of the ideas generated by the "why" and "how" discussions are worth pursuing.

There are other types of questions that show humility and vulnerability and help build trust. For instance, "help me understand" is a way to show sincere interest in the knowledge another person has. "How can I help" demonstrates to the follower that the leader is focused on them first. So does "what's the biggest challenge you are facing?" Starting a question with "I wonder" helps the follower know the leader doesn't assume they know the answer, but merely wonders what the possible solution might be. Asking a team member if they're clear on what they're doing and why allows them to admit they might not be aligned with the vision and strategy, something they'll be comfortable doing if the leader has built trust with them.

Each of these questions allows both the leader and the follower to be focused on sharing control instead of the leader taking (or forcing) control. When the leader has the courage to accept input with an open heart and mind, it creates an environment of inclusion by letting everyone participate in running the organization. The leader increases how much team members care about the outcomes because they are sharing in the decisions that they then base their work on.

Motivational interviewing technique

I have witnessed the power of helping team members get on board with their roles in the strategic direction of the organization by using motivational interviewing, or MI. I have even experienced the power of MI in parenting, realizing that my teenagers will be much more likely to follow through on a plan they have helped develop. I can also hold them accountable for behavior that is not consistent with their stated goals simply by asking how their actions are helping them accomplish what they themselves have said they want.

MI is a technique that was developed in the addiction recovery field. Despite being created as a tool for counseling individuals in recovery, it is applicable across many other situations, including as a collaborative method of communicating alignment among team members, because it strengthens team members' personal motivation for— and commitment to—change.

The basic premise of MI is that change can only happen when there is readiness. Bringing the team along and enlisting them in the vision is a way of getting them ready. Making change effectively within an organization requires followers to be part of the change: determining what needs to change, deciding how the change might be implemented, and implementing it while continuously checking back on how the actions are consistent with the stated goals. By using MI, leaders can help followers resolve any feelings of ambivalence they might have and find the internal motivation to contribute to change. The technique is founded on the idea that the more the leader tries to push their followers to make change because they "should," the more they will resist that change.[51]

MI is guided by four key principles:

1. Displays of empathy show that the leader understands their followers.
2. The leader supports followers' self-efficacy by encouraging them to believe they can accomplish anything together.
3. Throughout the change process, the leader doesn't impose their own viewpoint but listens openly to hear others' views while also rolling with the resistance that may come up by redirecting followers to focus on the stated goals.
4. When the leader identifies areas where the team's actions are inconsistent with the goals, they ask questions to discern where the disconnect lies and redirect the team to either realign the actions or revise the goals.

I used MI when working with my teammates on setting and working toward their annual goals. Each of my direct reports was asked to set goals related to their role in accomplishing our strategic plan, as well as their personal ambitions for themselves. Throughout the year, during our quarterly goal check-ins, we discussed how their actions were getting them closer to the goals. I worked hard to listen openly, but I also provided coaching when the actions weren't consistent with the goals that had been set. We then agreed that either the actions must be adjusted or the goals needed to be revised.

Vulnerability and humility are required to effectively use MI. The leader cannot push their own agenda and must instead focus on building rapport and trust with the team. They know they'll accomplish more by asking open-ended questions to encourage their followers to express themselves. And they'll reinforce trust with their followers by engaging in active listening, ensuring they ask whether or not they are hearing the feedback correctly.

Being the decider

When I was the leader of Women's Bean Project, I knew it was my job to decide. If left on my own, my natural tendency is to make a decision quickly and, well, decisively. Because I have realized this decision-making style doesn't leave room for humility and vulnerability, I have needed to learn the skills of information gathering, deliberation, and allowing others to weigh in prior to making a decision. I've learned to take a pending decision and turn it, like a Rubik's Cube, every which way to analyze the implications of each possible decision. Then I have to remember that, ultimately, I will need to commit to a decision. People are not inspired by a leader who waffles, agonizes, or otherwise avoids decision-making. There is a point when the leader must commit, realizing everyone is looking to them for their decisiveness, while also watching them to see if they behave arrogantly or in an overbearing way.

Despite trying hard to be humble and vulnerable while I was gathering feedback, I also learned to beware of teammates who believed that by asking for their input I was signaling I would do exactly what they suggested. Because of their role in the organization, the person giving input may not have realized they weren't fully informed of the big picture. They may have been making a recommendation that was focused on making their own life easier, not on what was best for the organization and aligned with the strategic goals. Or, they might—consciously or not—have been trying to exploit the vulnerability I was showing by asking for their input.

My job was to always be mindful of what was best for the company, which sometimes superseded what was best for any particular individual. If I did a good job of building trust, my teammates understood the tension I was balancing and still felt heard even when I didn't do what they suggested. For my part, I ensured I was clearly communicating that I was listening by reflecting back what I heard, even when my decisions didn't appear to reflect the suggestions from my teammates. Otherwise, I risked losing trust and leading people to believe my humility and vulnerability were really weaknesses instead of courageous strengths.

The leader who thinks their authority to make decisions means that only their own opinion is the one that matters is doomed to fail. Just as a parent rarely gets what they want from a teenager by demanding it—at least in my experience—a leader doesn't accomplish amazing things by demanding action or telling everyone the answers.

Intellectual humility

As uncomfortable as it is for many leaders, they must also have the courage to be wrong. They have to be humble enough to show their faults and be transparent about mistakes made or admit to things they wish they'd done differently. This includes being open to feedback and asking others how they might improve. Some followers only feel safe taking risks if the leader shows courage first, demonstrating they are worth following because they have made it okay to be wrong. The leader worth following doesn't ask their team members to take risks they are not willing to take themself.

A balance has to be struck between being smart and strong-willed enough to lead others to accomplish great things and being flexible enough to ask questions, think differently, and admit when one is wrong. This quality, referred to as intellectual humility, can be measured using the Pepperdine Comprehensive Intellectual Humility Scale. For the purposes of this scale, intellectual humility is defined as the "non-threatening awareness of one's intellectual fallibility"; that is, a person with high intellect is not threatened by disagreements nor overconfident about their knowledge. They respect other's viewpoints and are open to changing their own opinions.[52]

Intellectual humility can be thought of as the ability to sit between being open to changing one's mind and having the wisdom to know when one shouldn't. It has four components, including respect for other's viewpoints, not being intellectually overconfident, separating ego from intellect, and being willing to revise one's opinion. Intellectual curiosity and complex thoughts are related to intellectual humility, with high scores predicting open-mindedness. Interestingly, this quality is distinct from the virtue we think of as humility, which is about the perception of oneself. Intellectual humility means that one has insight into the limits of one's knowledge. It's required for someone to be open to new ideas. Humility, on the other hand, is much broader and applies to having a modest view of one's own importance.

The opposite of intellectual humility is intellectual arrogance. When I think of this characteristic, I think of Elon Musk. His recent purchase of Twitter (now X) and subsequent changes to the company's operations, policies, and processes smack of intellectual arrogance. It seems that as Musk watched from the outside, he became convinced he knew better than those who had developed the company and grown it.

Musk paid $44 billion to take Twitter private, eventually changing the name to X and merging it into a parent company called X Corp.[53] After his acquisition, he fired several top executives, including the CEO, and made himself the CEO. He laid off half the company's workforce, and then hundreds more workers resigned when Musk demanded they commit to extremely hardcore work to launch the new features he was demanding. He has been criticized for restoring the accounts of previously suspended high-profile people and suspending other accounts, including those that parodied Musk, along with ten journalists who were critical of him. An article in *The Washington Post* reported how X had "become a cacophony of misinformation and confusing reports" in response to its move toward conservatism.[54] A *Bloomberg* reporter also commented on the increase in misinformation and hate speech now found on the platform.[55] Post acquisition, X has allowed increased misinformation and hate speech onto its platform and the company has been valued at more than 50 percent less than the acquisition cost, has experienced a 30 percent decrease in active users, and a 60 percent decrease in advertising.[56] It's hard not to imagine that Musk's intellectual arrogance has contributed to X's decline.

Openness to ideas

A leader who is open to ideas, while not yielding at all times, is one who is confident in their knowledge and intellect but not arrogant about it. Their ego is not tied up with their own point of view, and they show respect for those with differing perspectives. This quality allows leaders to be agile.

Netflix is a company that has consistently displayed agility by being the first major disruptor, first in the home video market and then in streaming. Blockbuster Video created the home video market, starting with just a few brick-and-mortar stores and growing to an eventual 9,000 stores by their peak in 2004. Blockbuster was considered cutting edge because of their computerized video checkout system, but they also became well-known for their late fees on videos not returned within the rental window, which eventually became their primary source of revenue.

Reed Hastings was irritated by the late fees and founded Netflix in 1997 to disrupt the market by allowing customers to order their DVDs online to be delivered to their homes and kept as long as they wished without penalty. Blockbuster largely ignored Netflix, sticking with their original strategy until 2004 when they finally launched their online business. Netflix moved ahead of them again by introducing online streaming in advance of all industry competition. Blockbuster's lack of agility led them from being a market leader in home entertainment to filing for bankruptcy in 2010.

Much has been written about Netflix and their culture—a culture that allows for agility. One specific example is their rule around championing the brilliant idea your boss hates. This means that employees—even ones who aren't senior in the company—can research and promote an idea even if their boss doesn't like it. Hastings, now Netflix's executive chairman, says it's okay for an employee to disagree with their manager and implement an idea the manager doesn't like. Netflix leadership doesn't want people setting aside a great idea just because their manager doesn't realize how great it is. Team members in the company are empowered to make their case for ideas they feel strongly about because these ideas might have a chance at winning. For example, this philosophy led to Netflix allowing customers to download movies to their device for viewing. Netflix's senior leadership thought this was a bad idea, but two employees were able to conduct customer research and provide data supporting their customers' desire to do more than stream movies.[57] This shift allowed Netflix to become a market leader. Think about other companies where ideas a boss hates will never see the light of day as long as that leader is there. How many market-changing ideas have been buried or lost due to a leader's inability to listen to their team and lead with agility?

Kodak, a company known in its early years for its innovation (they once held over twenty thousand US patents) displayed little business agility when they were slow to make the transformation to digital photography. Despite perfecting the world's first digital camera by 1975, Kodak wasn't agile enough to respond to the changes in their industry. Instead, Kodak management decided not to take the digital camera to market because the margins on film sales were so strong.[58] As a result, they remained reliant on film sales, even as consumers embraced digital photography. Though they eventually introduced a digital camera in 1993, they didn't invest in innovation, so by the time film sales had dropped to just 25 percent of Kodak's sales, they were losing money on every digital camera they sold.[59]

When Kodak filed for bankruptcy in 2012, they were still producing film and had also shifted their focus to digital printing services. One might think this would have been the end of the company, but they eventually got their mojo back when post-pandemic popular culture revived the use of film. Some high-profile celebrities have returned to shooting on film, and the second season of the popular HBO show *Euphoria* was shot on Kodak film. It's hard to know if this renaissance for film will be sustained or if Kodak's lack of agility will resurface, but their year-over-year earnings have dropped, possibly signaling a declining trend.[60]

A hard lesson

This lesson in being a leader worth following is complicated. It involves the leader having the strength to say they know they don't have all the answers and need help. But it also means the leader doesn't think less of themselves—they think of themself less. Rather than viewing vulnerability as a sign of weakness, the leader who inspires others to follow must realize it really means showing the courage to take a risk, putting oneself out there and placing one's ego on the line, even when the outcome is uncertain and can't be controlled. It requires overcoming the belief that being a learner, not a knower, and asking good questions to guide followers to their own solutions is a sign of weakness.

Being a courageous leader requires intellectual humility and being familiar with one's own strengths and weaknesses, while not giving over to complete deference. It means the leader must be agile in their thinking and open-minded enough to allow for adaptations to the strategy based on input from the team. It is no wonder many leaders struggle with this aspect of courage; it is a tremendous shift from the old way of being a leader, but like all skills, it gets easier the more one practices it.

Do you struggle to show humility and vulnerability? Are you concerned it makes you seem weak to your followers? How might you shift your thinking to see humility and vulnerability as strengths?

In the next section we will explore the final characteristic of being a leader worth following: emotional intelligence.

Chapter 17
Emotional Intelligence

Like many companies in 2021, Better.com, a digital mortgage company, was adjusting to the rapid changes brought on by the pandemic. Shortly after receiving a $750 million capital investment, a last-minute Zoom call was scheduled on a Friday afternoon. When the nine hundred invited employees showed up for the video conference with Vishal Garg, the CEO, they were told if they were on the call, they were part of the unlucky group being laid off—they were terminated, effective immediately.[61]

Certainly, there is no easy way to do mass layoffs. But there are humane ways to deliver bad news. In this case, the Better. com CEO made it about himself. He said this was the second time in his career he had laid people off, and he didn't want to do it. He shared that the last time he did it, he cried. He showed no sympathy for the people losing their jobs, and he showed no empathy for the position they were in.

Perhaps the layoffs could have been justified if Garg had related the downsizing to a larger vision about how it was going to help the company change the world (because that is what the Better.com website says they are trying to do). Why would anyone on the call care about Garg and his feelings when he didn't acknowledge the feelings of others? Was he really so disconnected from his employees?

This wasn't the first time Garg was in the news. In the previous year, a memo was leaked to the media in which Garg accused some employees of being dumb dolphins, saying, "DUMB DOLPHINS get caught in nets and eaten by sharks. SO STOP IT. STOP IT. STOP IT RIGHT NOW. YOU ARE EMBARRASSING ME."[62]

After the poor delivery of the layoff news, Garg was lambasted on social media. He returned to the airwaves and apologized for how he had mishandled the situation. Part of his apology included the following line: "I realize the way I communicated this news made a difficult situation worse. I am deeply sorry and am committed to learning from the situation and doing more to be the leader that you expect me to be." Then, in a subsequent statement, he accused a number of the terminated employees of stealing from the company by working just two hours a day.

Recovering from a misstep

A leader worth following understands leading is not only about what the leader expects from their followers but about what the followers expect of the leader. Even though, after his initial gaffe, Garg did take responsibility for the impact of his actions, show sympathy, and say he was striving to be more of the kind of leader people wished he could be, it appears that attitude wasn't sustainable and perhaps not genuine. Maybe he meant what he said, though that's the problem for a leader who missteps. When the leader returns with an explanation, apology, or acknowledgment of the error, it can be hard for followers to trust that the follow-up is genuine, rather than an attempt at repairing their image. Followers will watch the leader closely to see if their subsequent behavior helps them recover trust or further diminishes it. Leaders who don't understand this not only let their followers down, they damage their authority to lead.

Self-aware leaders

Self-awareness, or our ability to see ourselves clearly, is a key to being a successful leader. There are two types of self-awareness: internal and external. An individual with internal self-awareness clearly understands how their own values, passions, and aspirations fit within their surroundings and how they impact others. External self-awareness is an understanding of how others view us. Essentially, the two types of self-awareness are the difference between how well one knows oneself versus how well one understands how they are seen by others.[63]

Those who lack self-awareness cannot empathize; they are unable to read the room and have a tendency to overinflate their own contributions and performance. Unfortunately, a me-first mentality is all too prevalent among leaders today, making these leaders come across as tone-deaf and insensitive. Like Vishal Garg, these leaders are hurtful without realizing it. Often they take sole credit for success and blame others for failure. Even if they do wish to be collaborative and helpful, they have no awareness they are falling short of their followers' expectations of them.

In 1995, Daniel Goleman published his book *Emotional Intelligence* in which he defined emotional intelligence as the ability to perceive, use, understand, manage, and handle emotions—both one's own and others'. However, merely recognizing emotions isn't enough. Thinking and behavior must be affected as well.

Leaders with strong emotional intelligence are able to identify and label their feelings correctly. They are aware of their own idiosyncrasies, which gives them the ability to understand what is happening in a situation that elicits certain emotions, making it possible for them to name the feelings and separate their own feelings from those of their followers.

When I notice myself responding strongly to a situation, I have found it helpful to first ask why. Is the new situation reminding me of something that happened in the past? Are my feelings really about the current situation, or are they related to that past experience? I find when I process my emotional response in this way, I am in a better position to ask myself what I would like to do about the situation in front of me and navigate the existing—not the imagined—social environment, or plan for what I would do differently in the future.

Leaders who are self-important value their own feelings over others' and show a lack of self-awareness. If I allow a feeling of self-importance to cloud my perception in a heightened situation, I will not receive or be open to the kind of good feedback that will allow me to build or maintain trust from others. Lack of self-awareness and genuine caring can repulse followers and make them feel that the leader is dangerous and not focused on their best interests.

Authentic leadership requires self-awareness because it is the healthy alignment between the leader's internal values and beliefs and external behavior. Without personal insight, how could a leader be their authentic self? How would they know where to start? A leader worth following shows up as their authentic, best self and honors the authenticity in others. One would think being self-aware and authentic wouldn't be a challenge, but according to research by organizational psychologist Tasha Eurich, 95 percent of people believe they are self-aware, but only 10 to 15 percent actually fit the criteria of being self-aware. Ironically, too much self-awareness can reduce one's self-esteem, making it more likely a self-aware person might not identify as such.[64]

Self-management and leadership

For an emotionally intelligent leader, self-management is essential because it requires the leader to assess and navigate difficult situations without losing focus or composure. The leader who has mastered self-management is steadfast when things are tough and enthusiastic and optimistic when those attitudes are most needed. They stay positive despite setbacks in a way that can show up as unwavering optimism in the face of adversity. An emotionally intelligent leader takes the information needed to improve from their experiences, while also managing their own emotions, especially in stressful situations. They are observant, not reactive or impulsive.[65]

A leader worth following often amazes us with their courage when they avoid making hasty decisions. Through their deliberate self-management they are also able to reduce the intensity of their and their team's emotions. They look at problems from a place of possibility, focused on why something didn't work, instead of the fact that it didn't work, while also exploring solutions and managing the consequences of the situation gone wrong. These leaders seem masterful at redirecting negative emotions and impulses, never jumping to quick conclusions and never resorting to finger-pointing.

One can often observe how leaders who inspire others to follow don't allow fear to sabotage their confidence in themselves and others. They never wear a defensive mask to hide their own shame, fear, or lack of confidence. We can identify the leaders who wear the mask because they boss people around, display false charisma, and work hard to command all the attention.

Leaders who have mastered self-management routinely ask themselves and their followers what they are doing that is working, what is getting in the way of their success, and what they can do differently or more of. Their mastery allows them to manage their own emotions and reactions, communicate better, be more oriented toward problem-solving, and more resistant to stress. These leaders avoid letting their impulses dominate their behavior, which creates calm and trust from followers. The leader who self-manages has greater influence over their followers to help them manage their own emotions. With this self-management, leaders make better decisions and more purposefully advance the team toward their goals. Only when a leader has mastered their own feelings can they become a leader who inspires others.

Socially aware leaders

Social awareness includes the ability to "read the room," that is, recognizing others' emotions and the dynamics within the organization. This can be challenging at times because the leader is often the last to know about the emotions of their followers. I found that people often behaved differently with me than they did with other team members, making it a challenge for me to be aware of all the dynamics occurring within the team. For instance, when there was conflict between two team members, no one would tell me directly, leaving me to intuit that there was tension and something was wrong. Once I asked, my teammates might share sparse details, but would be reluctant to "get one another in trouble." It was a fine line to walk as I learned enough about the conflict to coach the individuals in working toward a solution and remain neutral enough to maintain the trust of my team.

Self-management does not mean self-absorbed. The leader worth following is in tune with their followers and knows what helps them shine versus what can bring out their worst qualities. Leaders worth following take the lead when the going gets tough, taking responsibility for their own actions and never taking credit for someone else's work. They communicate clearly, with honesty and openness, as they share plans for the future, always making themselves available to address questions. They get a sense of the group mood and calm apprehensions as needed. When asked questions, they know they best serve their followers by providing information, clear expectations, and an honest assessment of the status of things. Proactively taking it a step further, these leaders check in with followers even when they aren't asking questions (or have not yet begun to ask).

Setting positive examples

Too often, leaders can fall into the trap of believing they need to be perfect to establish their leadership authority. But the reality of being a leader worth following is that when someone can embrace self-acceptance and develop a strong self-concept (a collection of beliefs about oneself), they will thrive personally and as a leader. When they have a successful relationship with themself first, they are better able to have successful relationships with others because showing the confidence and positivity that comes from a strong self-concept allows followers to feel psychological safety and comfort.

Showing gratitude is a way we can improve our self-image. Saying thank you sincerely and often is a way to recognize others for what they contribute. Expressions of gratitude make the person showing the gratitude feel more optimistic and satisfied and also less likely to experience frustration and regret. The recipient of the gratitude feels valued and appreciated and is more likely to trust a leader who thanks them as the leader seems nicer and easier to build a relationship with. Followers who don't feel appreciated may hold back from trying hard in the future, while those who do may go above and beyond.[66]

And finally, the strong leader knows how to apologize. An *Inc.* magazine article highlighted that a leader with high emotional intelligence apologizes well because they are clear on the intention of the apology. They start with the end in mind, remembering that the purpose of an apology is to heal a relationship. Contrast this with an apology that feels defensive. Genuine apologies are focused on the other person: "I think I offended you and I'm sorry" versus defensive: "I'm sorry, but. . ."

To provide a proper, other-focused apology, one must be empathetic and understand how the situation has made the other person feel. DDI, a global leadership development firm, proposes that empathy is the top skill a leader must have, which, as we just talked about, is developed from self-awareness and self-management. When leaders are empathetic, they develop strong relationships and resolve conflict effectively, even when they must have tough conversations.[67]

Empathetic leaders are more likely to act from a place of compassion. They speak candidly, with truth, humility, and respect for the other person. One individual I interviewed in my research for this book said, "My leader tore down my work but showed me how to build it back up again." Though the description sounded harsh, this interviewee emphasized they knew the leader cared about them because they described their own experience early in their career when they received guidance to make their work better. Not only that, the person I interviewed described how the leader was interested in them as a person and an employee.

A leader worth following displays a unique blend of charisma, vision, and character traits that attract people who want to follow. These leaders make us feel understood; we admire how well they read social cues and are in tune with how others feel and how they make them feel. Emotional intelligence is a currency that is valuable when we think about what inspires others.

Why would people want to follow a leader with high emotional intelligence? The most effective leaders are self-aware and emotionally grounded. They pay attention to their surroundings. They have a keen perception of themselves, as well as an understanding of how others perceive them. They are authentic, which can mean being put together and exuding confidence, but it can also mean showing one's faults. Too often "perfect" leaders are later revealed as flawed when a scandal exposes the gap between who they presented themselves to be and who they really are. Today we mostly want leaders to be honest and real with a strong sense of how they need to show up each day, how they are perceived, and the impact they are having on the team.

Leaders can be extraordinarily intelligent—renowned masters in their field—but if they don't possess emotional intelligence, they will wreak havoc with their teams, burn bridges with their supporters, drive down the performance of their company, and worse. To be the master in their work, the leader must be the master of themself.

Now let's delve into the four lessons of emotional intelligence.

Chapter 18
Give Acknowledgment, Recognition, Compassion, and Grace

A leader worth following provides acknowledgment and recognition and gives compassion and grace. They are conscious of how they make others feel and understand the emotional tools available to them to lift up their followers.

Acknowledgment and recognition

The most inspirational leaders are those who get down off their pedestals and learn about the hopes and dreams of their followers. When Jeff Immelt took over as the CEO of General Electric in 2001, he was tasked with succeeding the legendary Jack Welch. During Welch's tenure, GE adopted better management practices and increased profits. Welch was known to have significant financial acumen, but he also had a reputation for being hard-nosed and unrelenting in his pursuit of growth.

By the time Immelt took the helm, the company was facing an existential crisis. It was apparent to Immelt that he needed to convert the company from what it had become to a company of the future. In terms of business practices, he focused on increasing the agility of the company by adopting a lean start-up approach and freeing up resources to allow for change. He also spoke openly about the crisis the company was facing and the challenges he was facing as he navigated changes to GE's structure. He made sure everyone understood the importance of what they were doing to contribute to the survival of GE. He worked hard to inspire the team to focus on the future rather than the past.

An essential part of his strategy in enlisting his team was building strong emotional connections—a leadership style very different from Welch's. Immelt made a point of doing one-on-one weekend retreats with his senior leaders, focusing not only on their work but on their personal and professional aspirations. In his interactions with them, he worked to ensure that the team knew he cared about them as more than employees of GE. The senior team members were encouraged to speak openly and candidly about themselves and their opinions. In his meetings, Immelt allowed time for individuals to share their concerns and gave acknowledgment, recognition, and feedback specific to each person. By focusing on individuals, he created connection and enhanced his ability to see each follower's potential.

With his time and attention, Jeff Immelt demonstrated the power of acknowledgment and recognition in inspiring followers and building leaders. It is the leader's job to make sure that after every interaction with the leader, followers feel better than they did before. This is done by being more generous with praise than criticism and by showing gratitude with thank-yous that are specific and timely. The leader worth following knows everyone wants to be seen for who they are—that we all want to know what we do matters. Acknowledgment and recognition tells followers they are seen and that the leader believes in them.

What to do when it doesn't come naturally

Some leaders may recognize the importance of acknowledgment and recognition but struggle to give it. And when it isn't done, people become less engaged with the organization and with each other. They find it easier to leave for other opportunities in pursuit of a new leader that appreciates them more, even though the lack of acknowledgment and recognition usually isn't a reflection of the leader's lack of appreciation for their work. There are often personal reasons why leaders aren't good at giving recognition.

Leaders may fail to give acknowledgment and recognition because they themselves don't feel worthy. Or they're too busy to stop and appreciate their team. Perhaps they feel as though they aren't being authentic by acknowledging great work because they themselves aren't motivated by recognition. There are certainly generational differences in the need for acknowledgment and recognition.

A survey conducted by Gallup found that younger workers have a strong desire to be recognized for their work. They want detailed recognition given more often than an annual review. The survey found that 73 percent of Gen Z (born 1997–2012) and millennials (born 1981–1996) wanted recognition at least a few times a month, whereas Gen X (born 1965–1980) and baby boomers (born 1946–1964) were much more likely to say they never want recognition.

Because boomers and Gen X employees are more likely to be in leadership roles but less likely to crave recognition, they must set aside their own preferences. Leaders who don't feel the need for recognition are less likely to give it, which creates the risk they will drive away followers who thrive on it.

The power of recognition

If you don't know for sure what followers prefer, it's better to err on the side of more, regular recognition. But there are general preferences among the generations. The leader worth following understands their team well enough to adapt to their desires.

For Generation Z, recognition is what they are accustomed to in daily life. Likes and comments after they post on social media are the foundation of their interactions with the world. They are more likely to appreciate recognition that creates opportunities to be engaged with social causes, like time off to volunteer.

Millennials are also tech savvy, so using technology platforms to recognize them will resonate. In their case, if they don't get recognition, they may assume they are doing something wrong. This group prefers experiential rewards like tickets to a sporting event.

Gen X followers prefer recognition in private or with a small group because for this generation, public recognition can be off-putting. Rather than being positively called out in an all-staff meeting, they might prefer a handwritten note. They prefer work-life balance and the type of recognition most likely to resonate with them is extra days off or a flexible schedule.

Finally, boomers, the oldest generation in the workforce today, generally don't mind forms of recognition that happen digitally but find workplace rewards to be more meaningful. For instance, receiving a promotion or a nice office is more aligned with boomers' expectations for recognition.

This variety of preferences can feel overwhelming to a leader who is trying to determine the best ways to inspire their followers. However, leaders can't afford not to provide acknowledgment and recognition to their team members. Though people have different ways they want to get positive feedback, everyone wants to hear it. That said, the feedback can't feel gratuitous, like a throwaway comment of "good job." It must be specific and timely, and the receiver must feel that when the leader says thank you, they mean it.

Of course, these descriptions are generalizations. Not all Gen Z workers want public recognition, just as not all Gen X workers want private acknowledgment. When a leader is engaged with their followers on a personal level, they will be able to gauge personal preference and use the generational guidance as a starting point rather than a hard-and-fast rule.

Stay genuine

A disingenuous leader might give what they think is a compliment but is really just flattery. Compliments come shortly after the behavior that elicits the compliment. They are specific, offer respect for the other person, and give them credit for the job well-done. Compliments can more easily be given by a leader who is an active listener because they hear what is important to the follower. They come from a place of kindness, without expecting anything in return. But be careful: Being complimented about things that don't matter or don't have anything to do with work is not motivating.

By comparison, flattery can serve as an effective way to influence another person, but it is not genuine. Instead, it's a form of insincere compliment, doled out when it isn't really meant. Saying "You're awesome" as a nonspecific comment is flattery, but saying "That report you wrote was really insightful. I'm so impressed with the work you are doing" is a true compliment. Ultimately, flattery is a form of manipulation and serves to erode trust so that when the time comes for the leader to give a genuine compliment, it won't be believed.

Small moments have big impact

A leader becomes one worth following when they focus on building strong emotional connections with people. They can do this by walking around regularly, maintaining eye contact when they are speaking with others, and remembering little things about people, such as the spelling of their name, how many children they have, what they are interested in outside of work, or any other unique thing about them. Or, if working virtually, the leader can find ways to check in informally. Regardless of the organization's size, the leader sets the tone by modeling how to create small moments for the team members with whom they interact and letting the managers and supervisors know what is expected of them in interacting with and knowing their teams.

Overall, regardless of the company's size or number of employees, the leader is responsible for creating connection by knowing their teammates as individuals who have motivations and interests outside of work. When followers feel this recognition of who they are, not just what they do, they are more engaged at work, which leads to greater productivity. A group of people working together who are interested in each other's lives creates a humane workplace where people feel valued.

Every team member must know they are essential to the team, and the way they feel that is from recognition and acknowledgment from the leader. This doesn't mean everything must be a grand gesture—celebration of little wins and timely appreciation go a long way. The small moments of mutual appreciation for individual contributions create synergy among teammates. They also set the example for team members to recognize one another, which leads to forging stronger bonds and greater collaboration. When collaboration is prevalent, it creates better work outcomes, more trust, and a higher level of satisfaction.

Compassion and grace

Compassion is a way for a leader to show love for the people they lead. It involves knowing followers well enough to care about them. Showing compassion starts with a leader being willing to admit their own shortcomings and understanding how to be vulnerable and ask for help. It means the leader demonstrates they can relate to the human condition—that life is full of trials and all people want to feel compassion during challenging times.

The book *Compassionate Leader: How to Do Hard Things in a Human Way* contains data which shows that compassionate leaders have 66 percent lower stress than their less compassionate counterparts. They have 200 percent lower intention to quit their jobs and 14 percent higher efficacy. Followers of compassionate leaders have higher job satisfaction, are more committed to their organizations, and have lower burnout.

The book's authors also wrote about the idea of wise compassion. By looking at leaders who struggle most when trying to balance business wisdom and compassion, they found the hardest thing for most leaders is finding the courage to enter into difficult situations while being simultaneously empathetic. It's difficult to find balance between skewing so far toward compassion that empathy gets in the way of making difficult decisions and leaning so far toward practicality that the leader prioritizes results over the team's best interests.[68]

There is good news for those less naturally inclined toward compassion: Research shows we can train our brains to develop more compassion. Ways to do that include developing self-compassion, like seeing oneself as fallible and yet still lovable, and getting out of self-critical loops. Fully listening and being present and mindful when interacting with others increases the likelihood of being compassionate. It doesn't stop there. Go beyond listening and offer support or assistance, not because you feel superior to the other person, but because you can relate.

Compassionate leadership

Eleanor Roosevelt said, "To handle yourself, use your head. To handle others, use your heart."[69] She demonstrated compassionate leadership in her work to establish universal human rights. Though she herself grew up in privilege, she visited slums and ghettos, not to inspect them but because she could not feel content when others suffered. As a young adult teaching immigrant children in New York City, she saw poverty firsthand and felt motivated to take a stand against it, even though ignoring the issue would have been easier and forgivable in that time. Later, Mrs. Roosevelt was dedicated to the ideal of universal human rights and helped to create the United Nations.[70]

Eleanor Roosevelt's powerful convictions were reflected in how she called attention to others who were suffering. Many leaders of NGOs are driven by this same motivation. Though this sector wants to address and change injustices, it isn't the only place compassionate leadership can reside. Leaders can demonstrate their compassion in multiple ways. They can show up each day prepared to work on behalf of others, and even if they won't benefit directly, they can express empathy or provide support before it's been requested. They can also share credit and actively listen without judgment. Followers know leaders who show compassion can imagine themselves in another's predicament and are altruistic, not transactional.

Compassionate leaders seek to influence their teams in a way that helps followers accomplish their own goals. They approach life and their teams with an attitude of abundance, recognizing that everyone has something to offer and everyone is already offering something. The leader's job is to ensure there is alignment between the abundant skills of team members and the needs of the organization. These leaders ask questions like "What do we already know or have or do that could help us solve this current problem?" They approach their team members with a genuine interest in helping them thrive and have the wisdom to give followers what they need even if they don't know they need it. Often, this pushes the follower out of their comfort zone toward trying things they might never have attempted otherwise.

Rather than using their power to accomplish big things, compassionate leaders understand their role is to help others discover *their* own power. Leaders are also attuned to their own moods and feelings. They genuinely care for the well-being of their followers and often put others' needs ahead of their own by being mindful of what is going on in the lives of their followers.

Compassionate leaders are focused on the solution, not the problem, and provide coaching to help their team address challenges head-on and find and remove barriers to solutions. These leaders give credit when things go well and take the blame when they don't. They own their team's performance, whether good or bad.

Leaders who use their compassion to inspire others lead with empathy as well, being in touch with how others are feeling even when it is uncomfortable. They listen to understand the internal emotional patterns of their team, what gets in the way of their success, and what helps them succeed. They conduct themselves in ways that make their followers feel truly cared for.

However, there is a difference between being compassionate and making excuses for followers. The wise leader understands it's possible to compassionately hold a follower accountable and not excuse bad behavior. They have also learned to communicate hard news compassionately and with respect. This is probably most relevantly applied when firing someone because letting someone go can be done compassionately and with grace. When firing an employee, a phrase I have found useful is to say that their star will shine brighter in another role or company. I learned this expression early in my career, and it reminds me that just because someone isn't a fit in their current role, it doesn't mean they won't find somewhere else they can shine. Of course, the leader who chooses to say this must mean it genuinely, or it could come across condescendingly.

Giving grace

Grace is a gift of goodwill offered to another human without being earned. When a leader is seen giving grace, it increases the likelihood others will give it as well. Grace can be seen in everyday interactions as well as in times of challenge or crisis. Giving grace is one of the greatest gifts we can give one another. A leader worth following gives grace, and through grace, these leaders create hope in their followers. They understand and meet their followers where they are without judgment, maintaining a focus on what the follower needs to succeed.

Pre-pandemic, I don't think there was a lot of mainstream conversation about giving grace. Perhaps a benefit to the changes driven by the pandemic was the realization by many that we bring our whole selves to work. In 2023, as we were coming out of the crisis, I was speaking on a panel about the changes in the workforce that had been forced by the pandemic. I asserted that during the pandemic, leaders had to learn that we all bring our whole selves to work, and the key to keeping our teams intact was to not only recognize this but to embrace it by supporting our employees in the ways they needed by being understanding and giving grace.

After the panel discussion was complete and the speakers were mingling with the audience, two older gentlemen approached me to talk about my comments. They agreed they found what I had said to be interesting, but then one said, "But this whole idea of my employees bringing their whole selves to work—I don't know about that. I don't want them to!" Even if a leader would prefer a follower not bring their multifaceted lives with them to work, followers are the ones who decide what they'll do. It is up to us as leaders to embrace or ignore this shift.

Embracing this change will require us to give grace and acknowledge the pressures parents are under while they try to balance work with their children's schedules and needs, for instance. It means leaders will have to adapt and allow their teammates the ability to work flexible hours to account for fluctuations in childcare and school. Or it can mean giving a teammate time to move an elderly parent into assisted living and make the transition to caring for their needs. And it means taking the pressure off followers by being focused on outcomes rather than the amount of time they spend in the office at their desks.

Followership is about being human. Leaders worth following make personal connections with those they lead. They look everyone in the eye and let their followers look them in the eye, allowing them to see a leader who understands and respects them and isn't afraid to be seen in return. Leaders worth following ensure followers don't feel anonymous but are recognized and rewarded for their good work. They make it known that their followers' work has meaning to the success of the team and that they matter.

The next lesson explores the power of optimism for leaders worth following.

Chapter 19
Be an Undying Optimist

When times are tough, it can be difficult for a leader to maintain a positive mindset, but optimism creates a huge amount of power for a leader. Optimism makes leaders and their lives better. Leaders who display this inclination tend to believe there is virtually always something positive to find in every situation. They have a mental attitude that reflects a belief that outcomes will be favorable. Optimism makes leaders more inclined to adopt a coaching approach to their followers; they know how to get the best out of those they lead. Their positive affect makes them well-liked and well-respected. These leaders aren't moody but emotionally stable and predictable.

An inclination toward optimism can be found more commonly in those who rise to leadership positions than those who don't. A study of over one thousand US-based CEOs found that 80 percent were more optimistic than the average person. Leaders who excel in this area maintain a positive mindset even in challenging situations. They often model positivity to their followers, which leads to greater positivity within the organizations they lead—creating a positive contagion of sorts. It's important to note that optimism isn't blind faith but a reasonable belief that we have what it takes to be successful, as well as a readiness to learn from life experiences.

Leaders who maintain a positive mindset and outlook, even in challenging situations, purposely focus on their positive emotions. They have high self-awareness and high integrity. They are also good at resolving conflict and enhancing harmony among the team.[71]

The positive leader's leadership style means they work toward bringing together a variety of viewpoints and information to make balanced decisions while communicating effectively and building relationships with others. Optimistic leaders are able to paint a picture of their vision and inspire followers to join them, which then has a huge influence on the organization's collective positive outlook. Team members end up feeling their contributions are valued, they are motivated to help implement the vision, and they are more likely to maintain a positive attitude throughout changes occurring during the vision implementation.

The effects of optimism

Optimism is like a magic elixir. Optimists have a 50 percent lower risk of cardiovascular disease as well as better cancer survival rates.[72] They live longer and show lower stress because they expect good things to happen while also believing bad things can be overcome, making optimists better at coping with negative life situations. Optimists show more persistence, which means they are more likely to work toward goals and make long-term changes. They have a high internal locus of control, believing their efforts can affect the outcomes in their lives.

If there is a downside of optimism, it's that optimists tend to take more risks because they focus on positive outcomes, rather than the potential for negative ones. As basketball legend Michael Jordan once said, "I have missed one hundred percent of the shots I didn't take." Tali Sharot, a neuroscientist and professor at University College of London, has shared research which has found that optimists are more likely to create positive outcomes—probably because when they believe positive things will happen, their motivation is boosted and they try harder, which can positively affect the outcome. In other words, a belief in the ability to succeed increases the likelihood of success.[73]

Of course, optimism that is not bounded by reality is merely blind positivity. These two outlooks aren't the same. Blind positivity is the denial of anything being wrong, an "everything is fine!" perspective. Followers see through hope that isn't grounded in the reality of the situation or the crisis at hand. So, while the leader must project confidence, they must also acknowledge the uncertainty of the situation. Saying "we've got this" to the team when it's clear they don't isn't motivating.

Optimism's effect on others

I am naturally an optimist. When something goes awry, I often find myself saying, "Well, it could have been worse. We can fix this." I have observed how the optimism I express in my leadership has a positive impact. During my tenure at Women's Bean Project, it made the team more adaptable. We had a tendency to take most negative outcomes in stride and had a culture that believed anything was possible. I find others tend to listen more closely to my messages when they are framed in a positive light. The outcomes achieved when I led at WBP demonstrate that optimistic leadership is more powerful than the outdated command-and-control leadership style. We successfully raised money for a new building and exceeded our fundraising goal. We made it through the pandemic and adapted to the changing needs of the women we served. And, in March of 2024, we successfully secured the first $1 million gift to the organization. Our team developed an optimistic expectation of success and believed we could overcome any hurdles standing in our way. That's the power of a leader's optimism; it attracts others and inspires high performance.

Martin E. P. Seligman, a University of Pennsylvania professor, has made a career of studying optimists and developing methods for teaching optimism. He found that optimistic athletes, managers, and teams perform better, and more specifically, they are better at coming back from adversity and excelling under pressure. This is due in part to the fact that optimistic people expect favorable things to happen to them. Optimists generally feel good things will last and have a beneficial effect on everything they do, whereas when bad things happen, those incidences are isolated and won't last long. While positive and negative emotions affect the entire team, research demonstrates that leadership optimism affects a team's success because it improves their positivity as well.[74]

Upon Queen Elizabeth II's death, The Centre for Optimism in Australia published an article highlighting aspects of her optimism. Queen Elizabeth believed a better world could be built regardless of what conflict was confronted. As Britain recovered from World War II, she provided an example to the British people of how to behave with wisdom, dignity, and optimism. She was the epitome of the British value of keeping calm and carrying on. She seemed to understand at a young age that her role was to be a beacon of hope and optimism for the British people. During her seventy-year reign, she facilitated healing for some of the damage done by the British Empire, though not without generating some controversy.[75]

How to become a more optimistic leader

Becoming an optimistic leader starts with how you respond when things don't go as planned. When mistakes are made, optimists respond with concern and compassion rather than condemnation. They recognize we are all human and, instead of blaming, they focus on the fix. Optimistic leaders remember it's not what you do, but what you do about what you have done.

To identify possible solutions, the optimistic leader provides guidance to help people identify their best ideas rather than issuing commands. They ensure followers know they have their backs and often serve as a buffer between the follower and critics.

These leaders delegate well and allow followers to choose how they will implement the solution.

Knowing if you are an optimistic or pessimistic leader requires a high degree of self-awareness. Do you find yourself encouraging or discouraging your team members? Are your teammates energized or drained when they work with you? Do others leave their interactions with you feeling empowered or demoralized?

General Colin Powell, former US Secretary of State, had thirteen rules of leadership. When asked to share which rules were the most important, he said the first and the last. The first rule of leadership is "It ain't as bad as you think. It will be better in the morning." He didn't intend for this to be a prediction but an attitude to go to bed with. Powell's last rule of leadership? "Perpetual optimism is a force multiplier."[76] No matter how bad things seem in the moment, perpetual optimists believe things will get better. All manner of things become possible as a result of the leader's optimism because the qualities of an optimistic leader are those that result in a greater likelihood of success.

Not just happiness

Optimism isn't just happiness. Happiness is about how one feels in the moment, while optimism is about an expectation of good things in the future. The good news is optimism can be learned. By changing one's attitude and behaviors in favor of a more optimistic outlook and recognizing and challenging negative self-talk, a person can increase their inclination toward optimism.

It is also about learning to attribute success appropriately. Optimists have more positive attributions, believing they succeeded because of something they did: we succeeded because we were prepared. In contrast, pessimists are inclined to attribute success to things outside their control and failure as being their own fault.

When have you experienced the power of optimism on yourself and your followers? How do you respond when things don't go as planned? Is there room for thinking differently?

Optimists make more successful leaders. They influence their followers' positive emotions and inspire others to join them in accomplishing great things together. They also work to create a sense of belonging. Even when optimists fail, they acknowledge that the failure has taught them something and feel grateful for the lesson.

The next lesson is about how these leaders create an environment of belonging.

Chapter 20
Create Belonging

A leader who inspires others to follow understands how to get followers excited and invigorated for the work. When followers feel they're a part of something and feel they matter to the success of the organization's efforts, a sense of belonging develops. Belonging, or feeling accepted and respected for who you are and appreciated for what you bring to the group, matters. This is not just about followers feeling liked but about feeling appreciated for their unique contributions to the team. Team members who belong feel free to be themselves without pressure to conform to the group, other than what is required for working toward a common goal. Belonging allows a group of individuals to come together to accomplish big things. Team members recognize the work can't be done without them, nor without anyone else on the team.

Belonging is also created when there is a belief that everyone on the team is treated fairly, without favoritism for some over others. Leaders who play favorites create the opposite of belonging: a feeling of being an outsider for those who aren't the favorites. This results in followers leaving essential parts of themselves outside of work because they don't feel they can be accepted completely, and then they separate themselves from others to avoid the lack of acceptance. Instead, treating everyone the same but different in the context of their individual contributions is key to the team's success. Leaders who excel at creating belonging understand the difference between equality and equity.

Equality versus equity

The subtle differences between equality and equity are often misunderstood. Equality means that everyone receives the same things regardless of what they need to be successful. This can include having the same education or training for all team members. Equality can make a workplace more diverse and inclusive and help team members feel respected and supported because opportunity is available to everyone. Equity means that everyone gets what they need to be successful. When equity exists in a team, the individual contributors each feel like they can contribute to the team because they have been supported in ways that are specific to them. Equity makes followers feel valued because they feel the leader understands them well enough to help them succeed in very personal ways.

Because we are humans as well as leaders, there are people we naturally like more than others, people we click with might become friends outside of work if we knew one another in a different context. Leaders must overcome this inclination toward preference and find ways to express caring for team members that are applied equally. Preference can be shown in a variety of ways, such as providing extra mentorship or coaching to some team members and not others, offering more frequent praise or public recognition to some, or selectively including specific people in important meetings. Even if a leader feels they have good reason for these behaviors, what they serve to do is create a feeling the leader is being unfair and potentially discriminatory and makes the non-favored team members feel devalued and demotivated.

One way to show caring for all team members is to make a variety of benefits available to all, such as allowing for work flexibility as a means to demonstrate the leader understands team members' needs. This might include giving them opportunities to leave in the middle of the workday to take care of appointments or go to a child's school play. Benefits could include creating a suite of wellness offerings that are meaningful to employees— even if some team members value them more than others. Well-being benefits can show followers they are cared for and believed to have important contributions to make to advance the mission. Celebrating team members for their tenure, accomplishments, qualities, or characteristics can also help create belonging, including recognizing celebrations of traditionally marginalized groups like Women's History Month and Black History Month or making Juneteenth a company holiday. Each of these practices also creates a culture of equity because they allow individuals to feel valued in the ways that matter most to them.

The World Economic Forum has documented people's frustration with the prevalence of an us-versus-them mentality.[77] When equity and belonging don't exist, a feeling of increasing divisiveness seeps in. We can see this across sectors such as politics and religion, and this has, in turn, made people look to their workplaces for solidarity because work has the potential to be a neutral place where all types of people can come together.

In the post-pandemic world, belonging has become a top priority in efforts to attract and retain talent. People who feel they are part of something and their opinions matter are 27 percent less likely to leave and have 12 percent greater productivity. Teams who feel they belong stay together and do better.[78]

Ernest Shackleton understood belonging

In January 1915, Ernest Shackleton's expeditionary ship, Endurance, became trapped in pack ice while sailing along the coast of Antarctica. Though several attempts were made to free it, the ship became surrounded by ice and unable to move. The men remained living on the ship for several months until it was apparent the pressure from the ice was making the ship unsafe. Eventually, the Endurance was crushed entirely and sank.

The crew was isolated with no means of communicating their need for help to the outside world. Shackleton knew it was up to him to keep his crew from becoming demoralized. Though his big-picture goal was to keep his men physically safe until they could be rescued, he also knew their mental health was paramount. He encouraged them to socialize after dinner and led group activities such as dancing to keep the men engaged. Shackleton called this mental medicine; it fostered camaraderie and belonging among the crew and generally made the hardship of being trapped by the ice bearable. He also managed men who were potential disrupters by keeping them close and enlisting them in solutions so they wouldn't spread negative energy. While he took full responsibility for their situation, he never shared his concerns openly, and consistently focused on the future.[79]

Three lifeboats had been saved from the Endurance and the men used them to travel across the ice to the open water and reach Elephant Island. From there, Shackleton and five others sailed one lifeboat to South Georgia to find rescuers. The remaining men were rescued at the end of August 1916. The entire crew survived.

Being a part of something

Some of Shackleton's success as a leader was likely because he and his crew were attempting to reach the South Pole, something few people had accomplished at the time. To this day, followers want to believe there is a reason for their work, which is why we are seeing an increased desire in workers to be part of purpose-driven companies. The leader worth following makes it clear through their words and actions that their team members' efforts matter; for example, they tie success back to specific contributions, and they celebrate success collectively. This allows people to feel excited and invigorated by the work because they can connect their individual efforts to things that matter to the team. At the

Bean Project, we all had clarity that our work, regardless of our positions, was to create a place where women who wanted to change their lives could come for the support they needed. The work of the organization was not about any of us as individuals but a collective force to help advance our mission.

Leaders who understand their followers' desires to have purpose help them see the future that might be possible when the team works toward a shared vision. As mentioned in Chapter 2, team strength gets created when a group of individuals is enlisted to work on a shared vision. When a higher purpose than individual gain is felt, the team members go from each doing their own jobs to a collective of people working together to accomplish a larger purpose because they belong to something greater than themselves. Trust and comfort with one another develops, leading to deep and meaningful relationships being created among teammates. When people feel this type of connection, they take care of and help each other. They recognize and appreciate each other for who they are and do their best work for one another.

The difference between nice and kind

Sometimes a leader believes a culture of niceness is how belonging is created. While a leader worth following cares about their followers and lets them know that, being nice is not the answer. Nice people are polite and enjoyable to be around because they don't cause problems. *Nice* is a term that can be used when someone is harmless or basically average. But niceness is selfish. What nice leaders don't realize is that their concern with being nice is really a focus on creating a favorable impression of themselves to others.

Instead, a leader who wants to show their followers they care should strive for kindness, which is focused on the other person. The Dalai Lama said, "Be kind whenever possible. It is always possible."[80] Kindness is defined as having, showing, or proceeding from benevolence. It requires the leader to act with no expectation of a reward. For instance, a kind leader shows they care by providing feedback that is hard to hear but will be beneficial to the recipient in the long run, even if it may not be viewed as nice. The kind leader is generous with their time, their feedback, and their grace. As Brené Brown, says in her book *Dare to Lead*, "Clear is kind. Unclear is unkind."[81]

Creating belonging remotely

In today's remote work environment, technology makes team members accessible to one another, but leaves room for misinterpretation. I recall during the pandemic when we initially were forced to use virtual means for our meetings, I felt lost in my ability to connect with others. I realized how much I relied on nonverbal cues and on the "feeling" of the room to guide me. Like Spider Man, I felt as though my spidey sense had been taken away. For a while, I found it hard to lead while I was learning to be more cognizant of the tone in my email and text communications.

In time, I observed plenty of examples when communication was done poorly and created damage to team member cohesion. For instance, red flags came out when someone used ALL CAPS to make their point or chose words that came across as aggressive, passive-aggressive, or blaming. Using excessive punctuation, such as multiple question marks or exclamation points, was another way people struggled in their virtual communication. In the short run, relationships were strained as we navigated the new norms and learned ways to rebuild belonging. When we were unable to be together to interact in both casual and intentional ways, our communication had to adapt. Until we learned to do a better job of communicating with one another, our feeling of belonging to the same team suffered.

Like many companies, our focus moved to creating trust in this new virtual environment so team members would feel welcome to share their opinions. We started by allowing team members to share their feelings anonymously. We then made sure to reflect back to the team what was shared in a way that made it clear there would be no retribution or retaliation for negative feedback. Instead, all feedback was valued, and this value was reinforced when we asked the team to help create the plan for ways to address the challenges they had helped identify.

Communicating with followers in a way that helps them know their feedback is heard is essential to showing care for them. Only 30 percent of employees feel their opinions count.[82] They are always watching leaders to see what they will do to make them feel their opinions do or don't matter. Just as followers need to see how their input is reflected in the creation of the vision, they also need to see they are valued for their feedback, even when it is negative. When the leader makes room for team members to hear from one another and learn together, they grow together, and belonging is created.

The Thunderbird Airshow Team

Nicole Malachowski, retired US Air Force officer and the first female pilot selected to fly as part of the US Air Force Air Demonstration Squad notes that within her team, teammates were dependent on each other for their safety. As such, they would always stop to help one another, as outlined in their Wingman Contract. The contract represents an inherent and often unspoken promise the pilots make to each other that their actions will always represent the mission, professional standards, and values of the whole team. It allows individuals to always make decisions aligned with the team's goals and collective best interests.

Malachowski and her team knew they would hold each other and themselves accountable to the standards of the team. They had a culture of compassion and caring among the teammates. The Wingman Contract created belonging and, while not documented, it was understood through training and working together and became a promise the pilots made to one another. This shows that team agreements don't have to be written, but when understood, they create belonging among the team.[83]

What ways of creating belonging have you experienced with other leaders in your career? What have you done? What do you think works best in creating belonging within a team? How does your own emotional intelligence impact your ability to create belonging within your team?

A leader focused on creating a culture of belonging will build strong, interdependent teams. Belonging means team members are part of something bigger than themselves and feel like they matter, are cared for, and get what they need to succeed.

The final lesson of emotional intelligence may be the strongest tool a leader has in their toolbox: a leader who is calm can bring followers to great things.

Chapter 21
Be the Calmest Person in the Room

This final lesson of emotional intelligence is about managing oneself rather than others, i.e., controlling one's own emotions. The Edelman Trust Barometer, discussed in the introduction, shows that people want and need calm authority from their leaders. This can only happen when a leader has the ability to recognize and regulate their emotions during their interactions with others. Four capabilities are a part of emotional intelligence: self-awareness, self-management, social awareness, and relationship management.[84]

General Colin Powell shared what he learned in the infantry during his leadership training. He said no matter how hungry, tired, or overwhelmed you are, you must never appear that way to your followers. According to Powell, when a leader manages their emotions, the followers will follow the leader's direction, even if they're just curious to see what might happen next. While in his training, General Powell learned that how a leader shows up each day sends a message to their followers. Though there are some exceptions, in general, appearing physically and mentally neat and organized and operating from a place of personal control can show followers the leader knows how to focus their attention outwardly because their internal world is handled.[85]

Leaders can be smart in their fields and well-known, or even revered, for their knowledge but without emotional regulation, they will wreak havoc on their teams, burn bridges, and prevent progress in working toward the mission and vision. We have all witnessed people who can't get off their soapbox or don't read the room well enough to notice they have lost their audience. Perhaps they show disdain for people who disagree with them or avoid sharing their feelings openly and instead choose a passive-aggressive approach. Everyone knows they are upset, but they won't say why. These behaviors are markers of leaders who cannot control, or are afraid of, their emotions. They may also be leaders who are unable to identify or won't acknowledge their emotions. The leader is struggling to be in touch with how they are feeling and how that affects their leadership.

How to become more emotionally regulated

Emotional regulation is the ability to effectively manage and respond to an emotional experience. For leaders who struggle with emotional regulation, there are practices that can help them improve and begin to exert control over their emotional states. Increasing mindfulness is a good place to start.

Mindfulness is the ability to be fully present, aware of one's surroundings and responses to stimuli without allowing distraction.

It requires a nonjudgmental approach to the environment—noticing but not reacting. This includes not thinking about the future or the past and getting away from moving through the day on autopilot, without thought or intention.

Emotional regulation starts with getting into the habit of noticing one's emotions through mindfulness and asking "How am I really feeling right now?" Beyond that, it requires one to truly feel the feelings, not just notice and push them away. A person might realize they feel irritation and react by lashing out at others whether they are the cause or not. An individual practicing mindfulness and self-regulation will notice the irritation and ask themself what is underneath the emotional response. Perhaps the emotion comes from frustration with being reliant on a teammate for their work before a project can be completed. It can then be helpful to ask if the irritation comes from a place of fear. Maybe the irritation is really a response to feeling anxious about depending on another person for one's own success, and behind the anxiety is fear of losing one's job.

Once the underlying emotion and the root cause of that emotion are identified, the person working toward emotional regulation tries to move on from the feeling while also noticing the patterns that have come from heightened emotions. What types of situations tend to trigger these emotions? Is there a time of day when these emotions are more likely or certain people who tend to trigger them? What is their body doing? Is it tense? Do they feel low energy or the need for a mental break? Fundamentally, a leader can only model calm if they have enough self-awareness of their triggers for heightened emotions and a plan for what to do when they are triggered. And they need to learn to effectively manage their response and be willing to let the emotion go.

Meditation as a practice

Building a meditation practice is another way to improve emotional regulation. Dan Harris was a prime-time reporter for ABC News when he had a panic attack on live television. In response, he started a journey of meditation, eventually writing two books, *10% Happier* and *Meditation for Fidgety Skeptics*. As Harris was exploring meditation, he learned the path to calmness was overcoming his inner narrator, the voice in his mind that could control his perception of himself and situations, which was getting in the way of productive actions. He began to understand the state he had been in prior to the on-air panic attack: an inability to focus, being quick to anger, and having doubts about his capabilities. Through meditation, he learned to notice the feelings but not judge them and developed a sense of calm and inner peace that extended beyond the meditation session itself.

The beauty of meditation, even when only a brief daily practice, is that it can improve self-awareness, reduce anxiety and stress, enhance one's mood and attention span, and even boost cognitive skills. Research also shows it can improve sleep and overall health. I personally fell into the fidgety skeptic camp before I started a meditation practice. Though I typically spend just ten minutes each morning meditating, I find it creates a foundation for maintaining calm during stressful situations throughout the day. The combination of stilling my mind, along with box breathing—breathing in for four counts, holding for four, breathing out for four, and holding for four—allows me to reengage calm when needed.

Meditation doesn't necessarily need to be practiced while seated and still. Walking, doing yoga, stretching, or even spending time regulating one's breathing can be forms of meditation that will pay dividends later. When a leader needs to work through their emotions and regulate them, having a foundation of calm that comes from meditation is invaluable. Being the calmest person in the room starts with taking care of oneself first, akin to the instructions parents receive on an airplane. In case of emergency, if oxygen masks drop from the ceiling of the plane, we are always instructed to place ours on ourselves first before attending to others. This is good instruction for the leader as well.

What to do in real time

To maintain calm under pressure or in an emotionally charged situation, a leader must stay composed, breathe, and pay attention to their body. What is their body doing? Has their posture changed under pressure? What nonverbal cues are they sending to others? A scowl? Clenched fists? Followers will pick up on and respond to the nonverbal emotional cues of the leader. The leader must be conscious of their own bodies, starting by relaxing their face, shoulders, and hands.

Once the body is neutralized, the brain has the opportunity to identify the source of the stress response and choose to view the situation differently, or neutrally. In my experience, it is then helpful to work to reframe the scenario in my mind by asking what it is about this situation that is triggering emotions for me. What has happened in the past or with others that is causing me to respond in this way? Getting rationally in touch with these feelings is the first step toward feeling them, not pushing them away.

The next step is to stay composed as I continue to tune into myself and others in the room. Taking a breath to remind myself to be calm while I assess the emotionally charged situation is essential. This allows me to avoid being reactive and to exude a sense of calm and quiet confidence while I determine how to respond to the situation purposefully. It is possible the difficulty cannot be resolved in that moment when emotions are high for everyone present. But that initial moment of calmness coming from the leader will set the tone for the eventual resolution. Allowing a permanent resolution to come from a temporary emotion is a recipe for long-term challenges. By exuding a quiet confidence, the leader is showing followers that a resolution is possible, plus demonstrating what they expect from others in terms of emotional regulation.

Are you the calmest person in the room? Have you observed others who maintain calm even when surrounded by chaos? How might you improve your ability to maintain or find calmness? What practices could you adopt?

Leaders worth following watch their surroundings and pay attention to their inner worlds. They are conscious of being the type of teammate they value. They watch how others are responding to them and manage themselves accordingly. Calm leaders help followers feel reassured by projecting a feeling of stability. They are better able to avoid impulsive actions and to make rational decisions, even in the face of chaos or crisis. Maintaining and projecting a feeling of calm can serve as a powerful tool for leaders in inspiring others to do great things.

Conclusion
Become the Leader Your Followers Deserve

In this book I've shared what I've learned and observed to be the most important lessons for inspiring people to choose to follow you and accomplish great things under your leadership. Leading is a lonely business. My hope is that learning these lessons will help you connect with your team and allow you to build relationships based on mutual trust and respect. When a leader leads well, everyone is better off. The leader can see the positive impact they are having. Followers are more engaged, productive, and able to take on challenges. Everyone feels and behaves more positively.

We explored the difference between managing (something you do) and leading (a way of being). When a leader moves from a managing mindset to one of leadership, they can then also embrace the notion that how they show up—not what they do—is essential.

Throughout the book, we looked at four characteristics crucial to followship: vision, integrity, courage, and emotional intelligence. Within each, we examined the components that make up these characteristics.

The leader worth following knows they are responsible for creating the vision for their team, one that is well-articulated and reflects the company's values, and helps teams believe their work has purpose. In creating the vision, the leader must be adept at scanning the internal and external environments to create a vision that is relevant and audacious, and will change the status quo for the better.

Once the vision has been created, the leader's job is to enlist followers to join them and stay with them by both being the lead proselytizer and the one who keeps their eye on the prize of the better future. And finally, the leader must be the hopeslinger—the one who inspires others to dream more, do more, and become more with their message of hope.

To bridge the gap in trust that exists between followers and leaders, the leader worth following ensures they operate with integrity. This starts with realizing the importance of the words they use, understanding that their words have power and that followers pay close attention to what they say. These leaders know their role in building trusting relationships—making followship possible.

The leader also has the integrity to realize it's not about them and that allowing themself to be placed on a pedestal means there's nowhere to go but down. They also recognize their word is their bond, that they must do what they say they will.

Many of the followship lessons require courage, which can be a defining quality for the leader worth following. From being afraid and acting anyway to facing challenges—not without fear, but in spite of it—a leader displays courage. They are also aware of their own and others' conflict management styles so they can display the courage to address conflict in direct and meaningful ways.

Courage is required to stand up for what you believe to be true, even when others question or push back. This lesson is about displaying decisiveness and confidence while also maintaining humility and vulnerability. It is a lesson in balancing strength with the willingness to ask for help, feeling confident in one's knowledge, yet humble enough to know you could be wrong and admitting it when you are.

And finally, perhaps the greatest life lesson for a leader worth following: developing and displaying emotional intelligence. This includes giving acknowledgment and recognition for work well-done, and compassion and grace when things don't go to plan. The emotionally intelligent leader is the undying optimist. They know the influence their positive emotions have on followers and the power these emotions have to create belonging because, when it comes down to it, we all want to belong—to be part of something greater than ourselves.

Accomplishing all of the above while mastering one's emotions was the final lesson. Being the calmest person in the room will pay dividends in your journey toward becoming a leader worth following.

In the past couple of decades I've learned that leadership is not a destination. Leading is a privilege. It's about growth and continuous improvement—growing yourself and becoming a better human and growing your relationships by being someone who can be trusted to be there for the long haul. It requires a mentality of abundance that helps others grow, as well as a growth mindset for yourself. By pursuing followship, you are making a commitment to grow your understanding of what your followers expect of you and how you can deliver.

I encourage you to move beyond the ego-driven perfectionism where you ask yourself: Who am I if not the infallible leader? If I am fallible and egotistical, am I worthy of being followed? Here's the thing: you don't decide, your followers do. They decide when they trust you, when they are ready to buy into the vision, when they feel a part of something bigger than themselves. At that point, they aren't just following; they are in it with you.

This book is not a road map; it's a way of being. By now it's clear that followship requires a wide variety of skills and insights, including insight into oneself, as well as into others and what they want. More than anything, I wish I'd had these insights when I started my leadership journey. My hope is that I can help you avoid making some of the same mistakes I made.

If you'd like to further this conversation, please visit me on LinkedIn at https://linkedin.com/in/tamraryan to follow me or sign up for my newsletter at https://www.tamraryan.com to learn more about followship. You can hire me to speak to your group of leaders. I also invite you to email me at tamra@tamraryan.com. I'd love to hear your stories.

Acknowledgments

Writing is an extremely solitary endeavor. There are hours upon hours spent inside one's head formulating ideas before any words are put onto the page. Often, the people who influence those words aren't aware they have.

Special thanks go to Bill for his unwavering support of the time needed to write this book, and to Caity and Cade who inspire me to continue working toward becoming the best possible version of myself.

To the people I've had the privilege to lead: I appreciate your patience while I learned many of the lessons included in this book. I've been lucky to be a part of your journey as well.

I'm grateful for the friends and colleagues who allowed me to interview them and gain insight into their followship experiences.

And finally, thank you to the team at Big Idea to Bestseller who helped me shepherd this book to completion. Special thanks to Anastasia Voll and Carly Catt for your insightful edits and for keeping me honest, and to Mikey Kershisnik, whose upbeat support made the process surprisingly enjoyable.

About the Author

Tamra Ryan is a nationally recognized leader in the field of social enterprise and a highly sought-after speaker for topics such as compassionate leadership and social enterprise. In May 2018, Congressman Mike Coffman (R-CO) recognized Tamra's servant leadership and entered it into the Congressional Record of the 115th Congress, Second Session.

Tamra has received numerous awards for her work, including being named Most Influential CEO by *The Chief Navigators*. Other awards include recognition in the Ten Most Influential Women in Business in 2023 by *The Chief Navigators*, recognition in the Top 25 Most Powerful Women in 2017 by the Colorado Women's Chamber of Commerce, the Judith M. Kaufmann award for Civic Entrepreneurship presented by The Denver Foundation, Regis University's Social Entrepreneurship Award and Outstanding Alumnus presented by the Colorado Leadership Alliance in 2006.

Her first book, *The Third Law*, explores what is required for chronically unemployed and impoverished women to create new lives for themselves, focusing on the societal obstacles that must be overcome and the internal demons that must be squelched.

It has won eight awards for women/minorities in business and social activism.

Tamra received her undergraduate degree from University of Colorado Boulder and her Master of Arts and Sciences from Adelphi University. She lives in Denver, Colorado, with her husband, two teenage children, and two goldendoodles.

Endnotes

1. Oliver Cann, "Crisis in Leadership Underscores Global Challenges," *World Economic Forum*, November 10, 2014, https://www.weforum.org/-press/2014/11/crisis-in-leadership-underscores-global-challenges.

2. "2022 Edelman Trust Barometer," *Edelman.com*, accessed November 21, 2024, https://www.edelman.com/trust/2022-trust-barometer.

3. "2022 Edelman Trust Barometer."

4. Lee Rainie, Scott Keeter, and Andrew Perrin, "Trust and Distrust in America," *Pew Research Center*, July 22, 2019, https://www.pewresearch.org/politics/2019/07/22/trust-and-distrust-in-america.

5. "Warning Over Half of World Is Being Left Behind, Secretary-General Urges Greater Action to End Extreme Poverty, at Sustainable Development Goals Progress Report Launch," *Meetings Coverage and Press Releases, United Nations*, April 25, 2023, https://press.un.org/en/2023/sgsm21776.doc.htm.

6. Jim Rohn according to Goodreads, "The challenge of leadership is to be strong . . .," *Goodreads Quotes*, accessed December 4, 2024, https://www.goodreads.com/quotes/112552-the-challenge-of-leadership-is-to-be-strong-but-not.

7. "The State of Leadership Development," *Leadership IQ*, November 21, 2024,https://www.leadershipiq.com/blogs/leadershipiq/leadership-development-state.

8. BlueOceanUSA, "Simon Sinek People don't buy what you do people buy why you do it," *YouTube.com*, March 18, 2013, https://www.youtube.com/watch?v=UedER61oUy4.

9. Tom Huddleston Jr., "In 1981, this was Steve Jobs' vision for the office of the future," *CNBC.com*, October 17, 2019, https://www.cnbc.com/2019/10/17/steve-jobs-vision-for-the-office-of-the-future-in-the-1980s.html.

10. Walter Isaacson, "The Real Leadership Lessons of Steve Jobs," *Harvard Business Review*, April 2012, https://hbr.org/2012/04/the-real-leadership-lessons-of-steve-jobs.

11. Micah Solomon, "How Zappos Delivers Wow Customer Service On Each And Every Call," *Forbes*, September 17, 2018, https://www.forbes.com/sites/micahsolomon/2018/09/15/the-secret-of-wow-customer-service-is-breathing-space-just-ask-zappos.

12. Plasma Ben, "JFK - We choose to go to the Moon, full length," *YouTube.com*, August 27, 2008, https://youtu.be/ouRbkBAOGEw?si=Ahk-JBlBAr19VYaDn.

13. Kotter, "Change Management vs. Change Leadership -- What's the Difference? ," *Forbes*, April 24, 2014, https://www.forbes.com/sites/-johnkotter/2011/07/12/change-management-vs-change-leadership-whats-the-difference.

14. "Principles, practices, and beliefs," from "Practices and beliefs of Mahatma Ghandi," *Wikipedia.org*, updated October 4, 2024.

15. Rick Maurer, "Resistance to Change – Why it Matters and What to Do About It," *rickmaurer.com*, accessed November 21, 2024, https://rickmaurer.com/articles/resistance-to-change-why-it-matters.

16. Jil McIntosh, "True Or False: Did Ford Really Say 'Any Color The Customer Wants, As Long As It's Black'?" *Collectors Auto Supply*, November 3, 2021, https://collectorsautosupply.com/blog/true-or-false-did- ford-really-say-any-color-the-customer-wants- as-long-as-its-black.

17. Napoleon I according to Britannica, "Napoleon I: Quotes," *Britannica.com*, accessed December 4, 2024, https://www.britannica.com/quotes/Napoleon-I.

18. Dr. Martin Luther King Jr. according to NPR, "Read Martin Luther King Jr.'s 'I Have a Dream' speech in its entirety," *NPR.org*, January 16, 2023, https://www.npr.org/2010/01/18/122701268/i-have-a-dream-speech-in-its-entirety.

19. "What did Dr. Martin Luther King mean by 'we must accept finite disappointment but never lose infinite hope'?" *enotes.com*, accessed December 4, 2024, https://www.enotes.com/topics/history/questions/what-did-dr-martin-luther-king-mean-when-he-said-1136021.

20. "Relational Energy: what it is and why it matters to organisations," *The OR Briefings, oxford-review.com*, accessed December 4, 2024, https://oxford-review.com/oxford-review-encyclopaedia-terms/relational-energy-what-it-is-and-why-it-matters-to-organisations/#:~:text=Relational%20energy%20refers%20to%20the%20positive%20feeling%20and, either%20have%20no%20impact%20or%20drain%20our%20energy.

21. Emma Seppälä and Kim Cameron, "The Best Leaders Have a Contagious Positive Energy," *Harvard Business Review*, April 18, 2022, https://hbr.org/2022/04/the-best-leaders-have-a-contagious-positive-energy.

22. Kaye A. Herth, "Leadership from a Hope Paradigm" (PDF), *chairacademy.com*, accessed November 21, 2024, https://www.chairacademy.com/conference/2007/papers/leadership_from_a_hope_paradigm.pdf.

23. Jason Aten, "Before Laying Off 1,500 People, Spotify's CEO Made the 1 Mistake No Leader Should Make Daniel Ek sent a memo to employees explaining his reasons. It missed the most important point," *Inc.*, December 5, 2023, https://www.inc.com/jason-aten/before-laying- off-1500-people-spotifys-ceo-made-1-mistake-no-leader- should-make.html.

24. Marcel Schwantes, "Warren Buffett Says Integrity Is the No. 1 Trait to Hire For. Ask These 4 Questions to Screen Out the Impostors: If a new hire doesn't have integrity, you'd better hope they're 'dumb and lazy,' according to Warren Buffett," *Inc.*, March 6, 2024, https://www.inc.com/marcel-schwantes/warren-buffett-interview-for-integrity-to-screen-out-impostors.html.

25. PBS NewsHour, "First lady Michelle Obama on bullies: 'We they go low, we go high'," *YouTube.com*, July 25, 2016, https://youtu.be/-La-qOcO2aLU?si=JcOwejFjSs1XsdaZ.

26. History.com Editors, "Emancipation Proclamation," *history.com*, August 20, 2024, https://www.history.com/topics/american-civil-war/emancipation-proclamation.

27. "Abraham Lincoln and slavery," *Wikipedia.org*, last edited December 4, 2024,https://en.wikipedia.org/w/index.php?title=Abraham_Lincoln_and_slavery&action=history.

28. "Lao-Tze on How Thoughts Translate into Destiny," *HAC Bard*, *hac.bard.edu*, July 14, 2015, https://hac.bard.edu/amor-mundi/lao-tze-on-how-thoughts-translate-into-destiny-2015-07-14.

29. Arthur Brooks, *Love Your Enemies: How Decent People Can Save America from the Culture of Contempt* (HarperCollins, 2019).

30. Tom Vitale, "Winston Churchill's Way With Words," *NPR*, July 14, 2012,https://www.npr.org/2012/07/14/156720829/winston-churchills-way-with-words.

31. Caroline Castrillon, "5 Powerful Strategies To Build Trust In The Workplace," *Forbes*, December 18, 2023, https://www.forbes.com/sites/caroline-castrillon/2023/12/17/5-powerful-ways-to-build-trust-in-the-workplace.

32. Alexandra Liotopoulos, "The Story Behind the Mouse: Transformational Leadership at the Walt Disney Company," *Journal of Global Awareness* 4, no. 1 (May 2023), https://doi.org/10.24073/jga/4/01/08.

33. "Climbing to Success: Leadership Lessons from Yvon Chouinard," *Untitled Leader,* accessed November 21, 2024, https://www.untitledleader.com/lessons-in-leadership/climbing-to-success-leadership-lessons-from-yvon-chouinard.

34. David Gelles, "Billionaire No More: Patagonia Founder Gives Away the Company," *The New York Times,* nytimes.com, September 14, 2022, https://www.nytimes.com/2022/09/14/climate/patagonia-climate-philanthropy-chouinard.html.

35. Axios, "The 2023 Axios Harris Poll 100 reputation rankings," *Axios.com,* May 23, 2023, https://www.axios.com/2023/05/23/corporate-brands-reputation-america.

36. Warren, Rick, *A Purpose Driven Life.* Zondervan, 2002.

37. Gretchen Filz, "Mother Teresa's Humility List," *Good Catholic,* updated August 8, 2023, https://www.goodcatholic.com/mother-teresa-humility-list.

38. Jeffrey A. Chandler, Nicholas E. Johnson, Samantha L. Jordan, Darren K. B., and Jeremy C. Short, "A meta-analysis of humble leadership: Reviewing individual, team, and organizational outcomes of leader humility," *The Leadership Quarterly* 34, no. 1 (February 2023): 101660, https://doi.org/10.1016/j.leaqua.2022.101660.

39. Jason Aten, "Sam Altman Just Made the 1 Mistake No CEO Should Ever Make: The company says any similarity of its Sky AI voice to Scarlett Johansson's is just an unfortunate coincidence," *Inc.com,* May 23, 2024, https://www.inc.com/jason-aten/sam-altman-just-made-1-mistake-no-ceo-should-ever-make.html

40. Kim Crowder, "Viewpoint: Generation Z Workers Have High Standards for Leaders Amid Affirmative Action Reversal," *SHRM.org,* October 18, 2023, https://www.shrm.org/topics-tools/news/inclusion-equity-diversity/generation-z-workers-have-high-standards-for-leaders-amid-affirmative-action-reversal.

41. Andreas Rinke, "EXCLUSIVE Merkel defends nuclear power exit despite climate challenges," *Reuters.com*, November 19, 2021, https://www.reuters.com/business/energy/exclusive-merkel-defends-nuclear-power-exit-despite-climate-challenges-2021-11-17/.

42. Laura Paddison, Nadine Schmidt, and Inke Kappeler, "'A new era': Germany quits nuclear power, closing its final three plants," *CNN.com*, April 15, 2023, https://www.cnn.com/2023/04/15/europe/germany-nuclear-phase-out-climate-intl/index.html.

43. WFAA, "Ukrainian President Volodymyr Zelensky: 'We are still here,'" *YouTube.com*, February 25, 2022, https://youtu.be/wgCNKhtZYks?si=57ibvvidXkuZxxNZ.

44. Erin Snodgrass, "Zelensky Brushes Off Praise: 'I'm Not Iconic. Ukraine Is Iconic,'" *Business Insider*, March 1, 2022, https://www.businessinsider.com/-zelensky-brushes-off-praise-im-not-iconic-ukraine-is-iconic-2022-3.

45. "Veteran interpreter breaks down in tears after Zelensky remarks," *The Hill, Yahoo!news*, February 27, 2022, https://www.yahoo.com/news/veteran-interpreter-breaks-down-tears-182409302.html?guccounter=1&guce_referrer=aHR0cHM6Ly93d3cuYmluZy5jb20v&guce_referrer_sig=AQA-AALrI4YceOgfnZ6gI2AdDF5153o2f1D6WAjLRLj_scw9Oxih1KgSwBkyOl oLWTN8f_69X5V_KXpr-nahoWAcmbC0KQW7C1tFgwqcl1qifZ9oaBsV-t duYMjkFI6dqGzYtBtxS_LSGab81mL5-vkkMWKMCN2ygX3yK1fWPdt5T C243.

46. Amy McKenna, "15 Nelson Mandela Quotes," *Britannica*, accessed December 4, 2024, https://www.britannica.com/list/nelson-mandela-quotes.

47. T. Franklin Murphy, " Thomas-Kilmann Conflict MODE Instrument," *Psychology Fanatic*, psychologyfanatic.com, October 24, 2024, https://psychologyfanatic.com/thomas-kilmann-conflict-mode-instrument/.

48. Tom Popomaronis, "Jeff Bezos: Amazon turned into 'the everything store' thanks to an email to 1,000 random people," *CNBC.com*, October 8, 2020, https://www.cnbc.com/2020/10/08/jeff-bezos-amazon-turned-into-the-everything-store-because-of-an-email-i-sent-in-1997.html.

49. Tom Huddleston Jr., "Jeff Bezos shared a 22-year-old article predicting Amazon's failure to show how to deal with criticism, *CNBC.com*, October 12, 2021, https://www.cnbc.com/2021/10/12/jeff-bezos-shared-a-22-year-old-article-predicting-amazons-failure.html.

50. Taylor Locke, "Why Jeff Bezos never doubted Amazon – even with its stock fell to $6," *CNBC.com*, October 25, 2024, https://www.cnbc.com/2019/10/25/why-jeff-bezos-never-doubted- amazons-potential.html.

51. Reviewed by Psychology Today Staff, "Motivational Interviewing," *Psychology Today*, updated June 6, 2022, https://www.psychologytoday.com/us/therapy-types/motivational-interviewing.

52. Elizabeth J. Krumrei-Mancuso and Steven V. Rouse, "The Development and Validation of the Comprehensive Intellectual Humility Scale," *Journal of Personality Assessment* 98, no. 2 (2016): 209–221, https://doi.org/10.1080/00223891.2015.1068174.

53. "Acquisition of Twitter by Elon Musk," *Wikipedia.org*, updated October 30, 2024, https://en.wikipedia.org/wiki/Acquisition_of_Twitter_by_ Elon_ Musk.

54. Will Oremus, Elizabeth Dwoskin, Sarah Ellison, and Jeremy B. Merrill, "A year later, Musk's X is tilting right. And sinking," *The Washington Post*, October 27, 2023, https://www.washingtonpost.com/technology/2023/10/27/elon-musk-twitter-x-anniversary.

55. "Musk's Free Speech Mantra Collides With Crackdowns on Hate Speech and Disinformation," *Bloomberg*, 08/15/2024, https://www.bloomberg.com/news/articles/2024-08-15/musk-s-free-speech-mantra-collides-with-crackdown-on-hate-speech-disinformation.

56. Jay Peters, "Elon Musk's Twitter, one year later," *Way Back Machine*, web.archive.org, October 27, 2023, https://web.archive.org/web/20231027140756/https://www.theverge.com/23934205/elon-musk-twitter-x-one-year-later-acquisition.

57. Hal Koss, "7 Leadership Lessons From Netflix Co-Founder Reed Hastings," *Built In*, builtin.com, updated June 26, 2024, https://builtin.com/company-culture/netflix-book.

58. David Gann, "Kodak invented the digital camera - then killed it. Why innovation often fails," *World Economic Forum*, weforum.org, June 23, 2016, https://www.weforum.org/stories/2016/06/leading-innovation-through-the-chicanes/.

59. Ernest Scheyder, "Focus on past glory kept Kodak from digital win," *Reuters*, reuters.com, January 19, 2012, https://www.reuters.com/article/business/focus-on-past-glory-kept-kodak-from-digital-win-idUSTRE8OI1N1/.

60. "A Kodak Moment: Why Is The Camera Company Seeing a Comeback?" *cogsy.com*, October 21, 2022, https://cogsy.com/blog/kodak-comeback-explained.

61. "Better.com's CEO who fired 900 employees via Zoom call undergoes leadership training to win staff trust," *Business Today*, businesstoday.in, updated August 26, 2023, https://www.businesstoday.in/latest/trends/story/bettercoms-ceo-who-fired-900-employees-via-zoom-call-undergoes-leadership-training-to-win-staff-trust-395742-2023-08-26.

62. Jack Kelly, "Better.com's CEO Called Workers 'Dumb Dolphins'—Three Executives Quit," *Forbes*, April 21, 2022, https://www.forbes.com/sites/jackkelly/2021/12/08/bettercoms-ceo-called-workers-dumb-dolphins-three-executives-quit.

63. Tasha Eurich, "What Self-Awareness Really Is (and How to Cultivate It)," *Harvard Business Review*, hbr.org, January 4, 2018, https://hbr.org/2018/01/what-self-awareness-really-is-and-how-to-cultivate-it.

64. "What Is Authentic Leadership, and Why Does It Matter?" *Center for Creative Leadership*, ccl.org, October 17, 2024, https://www.ccl.org/articles/leading-effectively-articles/authenticity-1-idea-3-facts-5-tips.

65. Gabrielle Botelho, "Self-Management and Its Impact in Leadership," *hrexchangenetwork.com*, December 29, 2020, https://www.hrexchangenetwork.com/hr-talent-management/columns/self-management-and-its-impact-in-leadership.

66. Kaylene Mathews, "The Powerfully Transformative Habit of Saying Thank You," *City Lifestyle*, citylifestyle.com, accessed November 21, 2024, https://citylifestyle.com/articles/the-powerfully-transformative-habit-of-saying-thank-you.

67. Michael Shmarak, "Sorry Doesn't Need to Be the Hardest Word," *adweek.com*, December 9, 2021, https://www.adweek.com/brand-marketing/sorry-doesnt-need-to-be-the-hardest-word/?utm_content=position_5&utm_source=postup&utm_medium=email&utm_campaign=BrandMarketing_Newsletter_211210114516&lyt_id=1295822&ntfData=login.

68. "How to Do Hard Things in a Human Way," *Potential Project*, compassionateleadershipbook.com, accessed November 21, 2024, https://www.compassionateleadershipbook.com.

69. "Eleanor Roosevelt's Most Inspiring Quotes," *Marie Claire*, marieclaire.com, accessed December 4, 2024, https://www.marieclaire.com/celebrity/a11250/eleanor-roosevelt-quotes.

70. Emilio F. Iodice, "Lessons from History: The Remarkable Leadership of Eleanor Roosevelt and Why It Matters Today (Part 1)," *The Journal of Values-Based Leadership* 16, no. 1, https://scholar.valpo.edu/cgi/viewcontent.cgi?article=1439&context=jvbl.

71. Bruce J. Avolio and William L. Gardner, "Authentic leadership development: Getting to the root of positive forms of leadership," *The Leadership Quarterly* 16, no. 3 (June 2005): 315–338, https://doi.org/10.1016/j.leaqua.2005.03.001.

72. Ciro Conversano, Alessandro Rotondo, Elena Lensi, Olivia Della Vista, Francesca Arpone, and Mario Antonia Reda, "Optimism and its impact on mental and physical well-being," *Clinical Practice and Epidemiology in Mental Health* 6, no. 25 (May 2010), http://dx.doi.org/10.2174/17450179 01006010025.

73. Tali Sharot, "Affective Brain Lab" (homepage), accessed November 21, 2024, https://affectivebrain.com.

74. Catherine Moore, scientifically reviewed by Jo Nash, "Learned Optimism: Is Martin Seligman's Glass Half Full?" *Positive Psychology,* positivepsychology.com, December 30, 2019, https://positivepsycholo-gy.com/learned-optimism.

75. "Queen Elizabeth's Infectiously Optimistic Leadership," *centreforoptimism.com*, accessed December 4, 2024, https://www.centreforoptimism.com/blog/queenelizabeth.

76. "Collin Powells 13 Life Rules for Any Future Leader" (PDF), *reachingneweightsfoundation.com*, accessed November 21, 2024, https://reachingne-wheightsfoundation.com/rnhf-wp/wp-content/uploads/2016/12/Collin-Powell-Leadership-13-rules.pdf.

77. Nayef Al-Rodhan, "Us versus Them. How neurophilosophy explains our divided politics," *World Economic Forum*, weforum.org, October 3, 2016, https://www.weforum.org/stories/2016/10/us-versus-them-how- neurophi-losophy-explains-populism-racism-and-extremism.

78. Jim Harter, "Employee Engagement vs. Employee Satisfaction and Organizational Culture," *Gallup.com*, April 12, 2017, https://www.gal-lup.com/workplace/236366/right-culture-not-employee-satisfaction.aspx.

79. Matt Gavin, "3 Examples of Courageous Leaders & Lessons You Can Learn From Them," *Harvard Business School Online*, online.hbs.edu, March 10, 2020, https://online.hbs.edu/blog/post/courageous-leaders.

80. "Dalai Lama: 'Be kind whenever possible. It is always possible,'" *The Socratic Method*, socratic-method.com, October 8, 2024, https://www.socratic-method.com/quote-meanings/dalai-lama-be-kind-whenever-possible-it-is-always-possible.

81. Brené Brown, *Dare to Lead* (Vermilion, 2018).

82. Gallup and Workhuman, "The Human Centered Workplace: Building organizational cultures that thrive (PDF), *Gallup.com*, 2024, https://assets.ctfassets.net/hff6luki1ys4/2pmxduM90hYkM5nnmGhOos/2fc9341ea266f61aa8e35ffb82bc461c/the-human-centric-workplace-gallup-report.pdf.

83. Nicole Malachowski, "The Wingman Contract," *nicolemalachowski.com*, November 26, 2020, https://nicolemalachowski.com/blogs/blog-posts/the-wingman-contract.

84. Daniel Goleman, "EI Overview: The Four Domains and Twelve Competencies," *Daniel Goleman*, danielgolemanemotionalintelligence.com, accessed December 4, 2024, https://danielgolemanemotionalintelligence.com/ei-overview-the-four-domains-and-twelve-competencies.

85. ajjbpaca, "The Essence of Leadership," *YouTube.com*, February 11, 2011, https://youtu.be/ocSw1m30UBl.

www.ingramcontent.com/pod-product-compliance
Lightning Source LLC
Chambersburg PA
CBHW062126020426
42335CB00013B/1115